ŽIŽEK AND THE MEDIA

ŽIŽEK AND THE MEDIA

PAUL A. TAYLOR

polity

First published in 2010 by Polity Press

Polity Press
65 Bridge Street
Cambridge CB2 1UR, UK

Polity Press
350 Main Street
Malden, MA 02148, USA

ISBN-13: 978-0-7456-4367-0
ISBN-13: 978-0-7456-4368-7(pb)

A catalogue record for this book is available from the British Library.

Typeset in 10.75 on 14 pt Janson
by Servis Filmsetting Ltd, Stockport, Cheshire
Printed and bound in Great Britain by MPG Books Group Limited,
Bodmin, Cornwall

The publisher has used its best endeavours to ensure that the URLs for
external websites referred to in this book are correct and active at the time
of going to press. However, the publisher has no responsibility for the
websites and can make no guarantee that a site will remain live or that the
content is or will remain appropriate.

Every effort has been made to trace all copyright holders, but if any have
been inadvertently overlooked the publisher will be pleased to include any
necessary credits in any subsequent reprint or edition.

For further information on Polity, visit our website: www.politybooks.com

CONTENTS

The unrealistic sound of these propositions is indicative, not of their utopian character, but of the strength of the forces which prevent their realization. (Herbert Marcuse, *One Dimensional Man*)

'If I'd known', said one of my patients, 'I'd have wet the bed more than twice a week.' (Jacques Lacan, *My Teaching*)

PREFACE

The Dog's Bollocks[1] . . . at the Media Dinner Party

The following joke is not one that Žižek has used, but it nevertheless vividly encapsulates the paradoxically serious end of his frequently comic means. In the middle of a vibrant middle-class dinner party, the host's old flatulent dog staggers into the dining room, flops down, and promptly begins to enthusiastically lick its scrotum in full view of the now suddenly quiet guests. To ease the unbearable sense of embarrassment that descends upon the party, a male guest says, 'I wish I could do that.' This produces a round of cathartic tittering . . . but only until the hostess adds tartly, 'If you give him a biscuit, you can.' In this joke, the dog represents the obscene underside of any nominally 'civilized' occasion. Behind the veneer of expensive clothes/wine/food and polite etiquette lurks the crude reality of bodily gases and sexual organs that the social mores and unobtrusive background ideologies governing our lives are designed to cover up. To apply this setting to today's mediascape, the guest's quip of 'I wish I could do that' is the socially acceptable level of humour/ideology that conventionally serves to defuse otherwise disturbing situations. It provides discourse's equivalent of a lightning rod – to maintain decorum, an attempt is made to channel away a disruptive intrusion. By contrast, the hostess ups the traumatic ante. She extrapolates upon the guest's interjection to undermine his attempt to defuse the situation. As an analyst of the media, Žižek plays the role of the hostess. The acuity of his media analysis is reinforced by the surprise-effects achieved from mixing learned psychoanalytical and philosophical insight with filthy humour. Žižek makes us confront the true nature of those traumatic issues we were aware of all along, but have found ever more sophisticated ways to avoid thinking about.

Žižek's unique mode of uncovering the media's hidden political ideology is demonstrated by two testicular jokes he does use (slightly adapted for current purposes – see *Plague*: 46; and *Tragedy*: 7). The first is set in an Eastern European bar in which a gypsy violin player is moving between tables, singing. A customer is drinking whisky at the bar when, suddenly, a monkey jumps up, dances towards him, washes his testicles in the whisky glass, and then dances away again. The furious customer asks the bartender why the monkey did this, only to be told that he should ask the gypsy, who knows everything. When asked, 'Do you know why the monkey just washed his balls in my glass?' the gypsy replies, 'Of, course', and proceeds to sing a dirge, 'Why the monkey just washed his balls in my glass. / It's a mystery, at least it wasn't his . . .' The second, much more perturbing joke is that of a medieval Russian peasant who, whilst travelling with his wife on a country road, is waylaid by a Tatar horseman who rapes his wife. To add insult to this injury, the horseman demands that his testicles are held by the peasant during the assault in order to keep them clear of the dusty road. Once the horseman has finally ridden away, the traumatized peasant's wife is further shocked by the sudden glee her husband exhibits. The peasant explains that he is happy because he had successfully tricked the rapist: despite the order he was given, he let the testicles touch the dust. A typical response to these jokes might be that the first is mildly obscene but essentially whimsical, whilst the second is deeply offensive and misogynistic for the way in which it subordinates for a cheap laugh a female victim's trauma (a charge Žižek vehemently refutes[2]). A failure to see beyond the joke's offensive content, however, results in a blindness to the profound significance of the combined form/content effect of the 'joke-work'.

These two jokes stage two diametrically opposed responses to political events – those of the *conservative knave* and the *left-wing fool*. The fool voices opposition, but in such a fashion that the real effect of those opinions is to reinforce the very system he purportedly wants to undercut. For example, the making of 'unrealistic' demands within a democracy enables politicians to claim that the very fact that even radical dissenters are allowed a voice serves to demonstrate democracy's strength. The practical fact that the political system will never allow such radicality to go beyond the merely symbolic tends to get lost in the aura of democratic *noblesse oblige*. By contrast, the conservative knave describes the conformist right-wing thinker who cynically applies her intellect to justifying tautologically the current system because of its *de facto* status as the existing system (the sentiment contained within such statements as 'democracy is the worst political system – apart, that is, from all the alternatives'). The gypsy violinist plays the role of the knave. He takes a substantive question about a real problem (the presence of monkey testicles in a whisky glass) and sublimates the problem into a song. A practical issue that needs confronting and solving is turned into an intractable problem – the mysterious workings of implacable fate. The rape story portrays the role of the left-wing fool. In the context of Really Existing Socialism: 'This sad joke reveals the predicament of the dissidents: they thought they were dealing serious blows to the party *nomenklatura*, but all they were doing was slightly soiling the *nomenklatura*'s testicles, while the ruling elite carried on raping the people . . .' (*Tragedy*: 7).

This deluded sense of holding power accurately describes those who think they are dealing serious blows to Really Existing Capitalism's own *nomenklatura*. Even at its most critical, the media commentariat who purport to hold power to account are increasingly difficult to distinguish from the corporate apparatchiks. Opposing such accommodationist tendencies, Žižekian analysis exposes the cynicism of a Western media system in which natural disasters like Haiti's recent earthquake (the monkey's testicles in the whisky glass) are transformed into the lachrymose sentimentality of a Simon Cowell-produced 'Everybody Hurts' (the gypsy's song) by a music industry moonlighting as a philanthropic agency. Unlike the holy fool and the cynical knave, Žižek encourages us to *look awry* at the media spectacle. In the case of Haiti, looking awry helps us to reflect upon the decades of geo-political machinations that undermine poor countries' basic infrastructures and thereby greatly (but predictably) exacerbate the human cost of disasters that are disingenuously framed by the media as unavoidable acts of God.

Žižek rejects the Panglossian fake solace offered by those who claim to find reassuring evidence that resistance and empowerment still flourish in the heart of capitalism – the Pyrrhic victory of allowing the rapist's balls to become dusty. A latter-day Diogenes ('the dog'[3]), Žižek continues the philosophical kynic tradition of exposing power's pretensions by exposing the nether regions the powerful prefer not to think about. He acts out the Shakespearean role of Tray, Blanch, and Sweetheart, who barked their warning to King Lear that his authority was empty; he also shares with Brutus the sentiment that he would 'rather be a dog, and bay the moon, / Than such a Roman' (*Julius Caesar*, Act 4, Sc. iii). Žižek combines the quick wit of the mischievous dinner party hostess with her dog's ability to disturb those sitting comfortably at the table. So, now, to repeat the simple but rousing opening words with which I witnessed Žižek energize a crowded public talk at the University of Leeds: 'Let's do theory!'

ACKNOWLEDGEMENTS

Big thanks for the intellectual buzz and sense of collegiality gained from the diminishing number of people who still remember what universities should be about.

United Kingdom:
Leeds – Ann Blair, Ricardo Blaug, Ben Bollig, Allison Cavanagh, Mark Davis, Owen Dempsey, Sam Durrant, Ruth Kitchen, Elizabeth Pender, Nicholas Ray, Tina Richardson, Salman Sayyid, Derek Scott, David Thom, and Sylvia Watts.
Manchester – Tony Brown, Mathias Fuchs, Graeme Gilloch, Rob Lapsley, Tim May, Cathie Pearce, Terry Speake, and Theresa Wilkie.
Liverpool – Imanol Galfarsoro, *Izena duen guztia omen da!*
London – Richard Howells and Ashwani Sharma.

United States:
Prof. David J. Gunkel has been a constant source of support and guidance both technical and intellectual – *Vivat na zdrowie!*

Prof. Jorge Schement proved a fascinating and generous Thanksgiving host – *¡Vaya con Dios!*

Nigeria: Azeez Lukuman, a true gentleman scholar whom I am honoured to call a friend – *'Bí o ṣe rere yó yọ sí ọ e lára; bí o kò ṣe rere yó yọ sílẹ̀.' Ayọ ni o!*

Japan: Hiroko and Haruki Asano

Special thanks:
I am extremely grateful to Justin Dyer for his exceptional copy-editing of this text.
Gareth Palmer – for all the bad films and worse humour.
Sylvia Tate – for all her help, encouragement, enthusiasm, and endless lists of things to read!
Diane Myers – for all her innumerable kindnesses. Congratulations on the great escape, but please 'take me, I can see'.

Finally, I hold immense gratitude and admiration for Slavoj Žižek and his profoundly inspiring, pomposity-free love for the sheer beauty and addictive fascination of theory – *Hvala lepa!*

INTRODUCTION

'The Marx Brother', 'The Elvis of Cultural Theory', and Other Media Clichés

There are many great authors of the past who have survived
centuries of oblivion and neglect, but it is still an open
question whether they will be able to survive an entertaining version of what they have to say. (Arendt 1993 [1954]:
207–8)

Slavoj Žižek burst on to the international academic stage
with his 1989 book, *The Sublime Object of Ideology*. Highly
entertaining, he has become an undeniably major international figure in cultural theory who regularly lives out the
possibilities of Arendt's open question. Now widely read
both inside and outside academia in disciplines as disparate
as theology and film studies, he is distinguishable from conventional academics not only for the extent to which his
scholarship is informed by and applied to the media, but
also for how often he appears within its purview. He is: the
subject of a documentary movie (*Žižek!*); presenter of a TV
series (*The Pervert's Guide to Cinema*); a regular contributor

of journalistic articles; and conveniently viewable in a host of YouTube snippets. A typical Žižekian performance, whether vocally or in text, can appear as a discombobulating skein of conceptual threads. He is frequently scatological in nature – his sphincter-orientated discussion of the elasticity of theoretical concepts and his literally lavatorial examination of the cultural significance of national differences in toilet design are just two particularly memorable examples.[1] Beyond this superficial impression (one that is exacerbated by the media's soundbite-driven agenda), however, the following chapters will examine how Žižek provides a finely calibrated account of what lies beneath the surface level of a mass-mediated social experience – ideological processes paradoxically hidden by their very explicitness and natural feel.

Capitalist media form a collective system which is premised upon the dominance of the particular by the universal (the commodity is capitalism's universal, society-defining category). The individual properties of any individual medium hence tend to be dominated and suffused by that medium's role as a subordinate part of an overarching media *system* – our newly digitalized society of the spectacle. The term 'media' is thus deliberately used throughout this book as a singular collective noun, the better to describe the systemic qualities individual media are both influenced by, and serve to reinforce. Acting systemically, the media system reduces the innate tension between the general and particular that attends any act of communication. The key features of Žižek's compensatory critical analysis include:

- the consistently accessible manner with examples garnered from the mass media to uphold and illuminate the central tenets of such otherwise intimidatingly difficult thinkers as Hegel and Lacan, resulting in innovative new perspectives on both previously abstruse theory and everyday media content;

- the constant use of jokes and examples from popular culture to illustrate complex theoretical issues – the ultimate seriousness of laughter, or, as Todd McGowan succinctly points out, when considering Žižek, we need to recognize that 'the path to seriousness is strewn with jokes' (McGowan 2007: 66);
- a bracing, iconoclastic interpretation of the ubiquitous and deeply naturalized nature of ideology today – more than most contemporary thinkers, Žižek is willing to mine the (only apparently) obvious and prosaic in order to produce startling insights into the true nature of our media-saturated age.

Notwithstanding the unprepossessing media figure he presents at first glance, by dint of his sheer presentational enthusiasm, Žižek, with his unkempt ursine affability, has become an unexpectedly mediagenic embodiment of Freud's return of the repressed – abstract thought in a media age. Hirsute, prone to physical tics, and with a heavy, lisping Eastern European accent, he contrasts starkly with more typically urbane media commentators (see Chapter 5) and well-coiffured intellectuals such as Bernard-Henri Lévy.[2] He is also highly unusual for the ironic and reflexive manner in which he is prepared to engage directly with the innate artificiality of media formats. Thus, during: the documentary film *Žižek!* (Astra Taylor 2005), he conducts part of an interview lying in bed, wrapped in sheets, horizontally suggestive of the toga-wearing philosophical figures of antiquity; amongst a number of intellectuals interviewed whilst walking or travelling in *The Examined Life* (Astra Taylor 2009), typically, he is the one filmed at a rubbish dump (at one point picking up a piece of a discarded porn magazine and saying, 'My God, and you call this porn?'); and finally, within a *New Statesman* article, he is photographed lying on the ground, grinning with his hands behind his head, amidst artfully scattered autumn leaves (Derbyshire 2009).

The visual shock value of Žižek's physical presence and mischievous posing complements the radical nature of what he presents for our consideration; whether he is talking about Homer's Springfield or Ithaca, Žižek's *joie de théorie* is infectious. He stands out forcefully from the standard media commentariat in his unrivalled ability to express scholarship-infused thought within the intellectual constraints of various media formats. Whilst being conscious of the need to avoid indulging in 'the reverse racism which celebrates the exotic authenticity of the Balkan Other, as in the notion of the Serbs who, in contrast to inhibited, anaemic Western Europeans, still exhibit a prodigious lust for life' (*Fragile Absolute*: 5), it is still necessary to appreciate the value of Žižek's vivacious scholastic engagement with mass culture and the full extent to which it goes against the grain of the conventional intellectual, throwing into sharp relief academics' more usual 'curious passion for the mannerism of the non-committed' (Mills 2000 [1959]: 79). He skilfully avoids the common communicational failures of both unqualified talking heads who purvey execrably simplified theory and their flip-side – woefully earnest scholars who are not always averse to 'making Homer sound like balance sheets and balance sheets sound like Homer' (Davies 1996: 23). His success may appear to stem from his media-friendly 'antic disposition', but it really derives from his inimitable ability to convey taxing conceptual questions via a wealth of jokes, anecdotes, and shocking illustrations. As likely to refer to Virgil from *Thunderbirds* as the classical Roman poet, the latter's admonition: 'Dare to disturb the underground of the unspoken underpinnings of our everyday lives!' (*Violence*: 143) acts as a useful motto for, *pace* Freud, Žižek's psychopathology of our contemporary mediated life. The underpinnings remain 'unspoken' because of the way in which today's ideology is embodied in mediated forms with which familiarity has bred consent. Žižek provokes us into taking a fresh, much more critical, look at the consensually over-familiar.

Žižek's willingness to engage with the mass media through a spate of personal appearances and topical journalism, even when unsuccessful, demonstrates an edifying commitment to Samuel Beckett's maxim from *Worstward Ho*: 'Try again. Fail again. Fail better' (cited in *Lost Causes*: 210). In his best performances the audience enjoys a Damascene revelation about something they didn't realize they knew about all along. In his worst, when his cascading thoughts are circumscribed by the media's grammar, one is left with an almost equally instructive sense of what pre/proscriptive formats castrate as part of their natural mode of operation. In stark contrast to contemporary anti-intellectual versions of Hamlet's 'There are more things in heaven and earth . . . Than are dreamt of in your philosophy' (Act I, Sc. v) as well as the countervailing tendency of those po-faced intellectuals who view popular culture as a 'sterile promontory', Žižek, full of strategically focused mirth, uses theory to tarry with the only apparently mundane content of our mediated lives. Resourcefully using the culture industry's detritus, like Freud, Žižek recognizes that the creators of fiction 'are valuable allies and their evidence is to be prized highly, for they are apt to know a whole host of things between heaven and earth of which our philosophy has not yet let us dream' (Strachey in Freud 2003 [1899–1919]: viii). The indisputably entertaining nature of Žižek's project repays deeper consideration – if only to exorcize such tired and facile ghosts as 'The Marx Brother' and 'The Elvis of Cultural Theory'.

1

THE MEDIATED IMP OF THE PERVERSE

INTRODUCTION: THEORETICAL SHORT-CIRCUITS

The *depth* which Spirit brings forth from within . . . and the *ignorance* of this consciousness above what it is really saying, are the same conjunction of the high and the low which, in the living being, Nature naively expresses when it combines the organ of its highest fulfilment, the organ of generation, with the organ of urination. (Hegel 1977 [1807]: 210)

The highest and the lowest are always closest to each other in the sphere of sexuality: 'vom Himmel durch die Welt zur Hölle'.[1] (Freud 2001c [1901–5]: 161–2)

Žižek's self-styled notion of perverted analysis is manifested in the title of his UK TV documentary series *The Pervert's Guide To Cinema* (Sophie Fiennes 2006). The fact that Žižek's analysis of the contemporary mediascape is laden with perverse jokes and topical examples creates the risk that its deeply serious political and philosophical importance will be obscured and displaced by a knee-jerk misunderstanding of the theoretical importance of perversion. Like Hegel and Freud above, Žižek recognizes the mutually constituting nature of the high and the low, and his conceptual legerdemain shifts between high philosophy/psychoanalysis and low culture to create sparking contrasts illuminating our normally unexamined, everyday assumptions (Roland Barthes's 'what goes without saying' [1973] and Gramsci's 'common sense' [1971]). This chapter explores the various ways in which Žižek's apparent unconventional perversity is in fact a highly useful method well suited to addressing the deceptively naturalized forms in which we tend to encounter mediated ideology. His use of obscene examples needs to be considered as part of his wider intellectual project, which draws upon a critical philosophical and psychoanalytical tradition to uncover the Heaven/Hell, high/low, dichotomies that structure our symbolic and psychological environments.

In Lacanian psychoanalytical terms, *perversion* is more of a technical than a moralistic category. It refers to a disproportionate[2] attachment to a particular ordering or structure of desire; as Karl Kraus so pithily expressed it: 'There is no unhappier creature under the sun than a fetishist who longs for a woman's shoe but has to make do with the whole woman' (Kraus 2001 [1923]: 13 n105). This attachment is typically manifested in the pervert's reliance upon a fetish, of which the sexual variety is just one kind. The result is that, in everyday language, the term 'perversion' has moved away from its original sense. It now tends to denote an exclusively sexual fixation – the familiar figure of the pervert who psychologically over-invests in highly specific substances/objects (e.g. rubber/high-heeled shoes, etc.) or highly structured behaviour (e.g. sado-masochistic domination scenarios). For the dedicated pervert, the fetish become desirable for its own sake. It assumes more importance than any overarching personal relationship with another person, of which sexual activity is 'normally' just one aspect. Žižek's patented form of perversion needs to be distinguished from this now standard association with highly specific, 'depraved' forms of sexuality. It can be better understood in its historical context; as Nobus relates: '... the term was appropriated by the medico-legal discourse on sexuality during the nineteenth century ... the term was transferred from its original socio-religious context, in which "to pervert" (from the Latin *pervertere*) meant to "turn around", "to turn upside down"' (Nobus 2006: 5). To the extent that Žižek is a pervert, he is an old-fashioned one. He is a theorist whose primary *raison d'être* is to turn conventional understandings upside down by the unremitting application of theory. The multitude of examples he draws upon from popular culture, no matter how entertaining, are all subordinated to radical, counter-intuitive theoretical purposes. He shares with Lacan a recognition that 'an essential step was taken in the present age when psychoanalysis undertook the interpretation of the fantasy in its very perversity' (Lacan et al. 1977: 14).

In psychoanalytical terms, rather than a pervert, Žižek can be more accurately described as a hysteric. The hysteric/theorist knows only the truth that knowledge is inherently ambiguous whereas the pervert (tautologically reinforced by his fetishistic practices) knows that he is correct. The pervert is thus '[t]he subject caught in the closed loop of perversion' (*Ticklish Subject*: 248). It is for this reason that the charge of perversion can be turned back on to those of Žižek's detractors who fail to see beyond the surface level of his obscenities – the importance of his theoretical insights is missed due to a perverted reliance upon disciplinary and professional techniques and structures. Whilst nominally more objective and rigorous, discipline-based (in both senses) scholarship tends to fetishize quantifiable data-gathering methods as the *sine qua non* of 'legitimate' understanding. In a conceptual version of Diogenes' physical acts of public indecency, Žižek routinely 'practices concrete universality by confronting a universality with its "unbearable" example' (*Parallax*: 13). Drawing upon Kant's notion of the *transcendental illusion*, Žižek considers the relationship between phenomena that are normally incomparable in order to create through theory an '*impossible short circuit*' (ibid.: 3). These short-circuits are valuable aids for dealing with the media's paradoxical problem of lost perspective owing to excessive closeness, or, as Marshall McLuhan put it: 'Whoever discovered water, it wasn't a fish.'

LOOKING AWRY AT THE UNCANNY WHEELBARROW ON THE DARK SIDE OF THE STREET

These photographs in the papers of children with cleft palates. I don't know what is precisely being bought or offered for sale, of what is being collected and on behalf of whom, but I'm so used to these eaten-away pictures by now, that when the other day I opened a magazine and saw a picture of a beaming and intact baby, I recoiled with utter horror. (Lewis 2009: 126)

. . . you know that what is already familiar is not exactly unessential. But when what is already familiar seems to you to leave a lot to be desired, seems to you to be based on a false premise, then it has very different repercussions. (Lacan 2008: 7)

Epitomized by book titles like *Looking Awry* and *The Parallax View*, Žižek's critical perspective upon otherwise deceptively self-evident representations encourages the reader to question conventional understandings of seemingly commonplace phenomena by viewing them askance. This produces the sort of counter-intuitive recognition contained within Lacan's above emphasis upon the unfamiliarity of the familiar and, in this vein, Lewis's sardonically provocative description of the sorts of photographs used in magazine advertisements for charities. It enables us to learn about something that was already (in this particular case, literally) under our noses so that we can avoid making the mistake of the security guard who suspects a factory worker of stealing: 'Every evening, as he leaves the factory, the wheelbarrow he rolls in front of him is carefully inspected. The guards can find nothing. It is always empty. Finally, the penny drops: what the worker is stealing are the wheelbarrows themselves' (*Violence*: 1). Žižek argues that Western media excel at using this sort of ideological bluff – the clever feature being that the ideological effect is felt in the very guise of 'non-ideological' media content. Pursuing this insight in a political context, one can see how the concept of democracy effectively acts as the inviolate background for political discussion in Western media discourse (see *Totalitarianism*). For Žižek, this inviolate status is suspicious; it produces in the theorist the need to develop a 'palpable critical distance towards the very notion of democracy' (*They Know*: xviii) . . . we need 'to look for the wheelbarrow which is stolen from the people when they are bombarded by claims that "things are nonetheless better in a democracy"' (*Parallax*: 378).

Despite the fact that Žižek follows the psychoanalytical method by often showing us something that we already really know, these are the truths we tend to be least willing to hear, a point that can be emphasized through a small digression on the subject of love. Falling in love is a process in which two individuals find each other amidst a sea of contingent factors – apart from relationships deliberately arranged by friends or family, most people's relationships start through chance encounters, coincidental work placements, etc. – only later re-symbolized as 'fate', along the ˄ lines of 'We were soul mates always destined to meet.' A successful act of analysis involves overcoming this tendency to impute false meaning and significance to an essentially contingent situation. In the psychoanalytical context, the tendency assumes the form of transference. In its positive form, the analysand projects feelings of admiration and love onto the analyst as an emotional reaction to the analyst's powerful insights, whilst in its negative form, the uncomfortable feelings caused by those insights provoke resentment. According to Žižek:

> The main ethical injunction of psychoanalysis is therefore not to yield to the temptation of symoblization/internalization: in the psychoanalytical cure the analysand, as it were, *passes through falling love backwards*: at the moment of 'exit from transference' which marks the end of the cure, the subject is able to perceive the events around which his life story is crystallized into a meaningful Whole in their senseless contingency . . . . (*Indivisible Remainder*: 94–5)

There is a certain contrariety in the fact that, in practice, empirically minded detractors of the psychoanalytical method have a paradoxically romantic attachment (transference) to a meaningful Whole substantiated by rigorously verifiable facts and figures. The resulting 'abstracted empiricism' (Mills 2000 [1959]) is of limited practical use when attempting to understand actual lived (mediated) experience within the mediascape. Freud saw those who resist moving beyond transference as akin to 'children of nature who refuse to accept the psychical in place of the material, who, in the poet's words, are accessible only to the "logic of soup, with dumplings for arguments"' (Freud 2001e [1911–13]: 166–7). Likewise, Lacan is dismissive of the self-defeating nature of 'rigorous methods' that are hamstrung by their own passive reactivity: 'When thought is not too empirical, it does not consist in standing and gaping, and waiting for inspiration to come from the facts' (Lacan 2008: 47).

There is an irony in the fact that the unpopularity of psychoanalysis amongst empiricists is a largely emotional, (negative) transference-based response, whilst psychoanalysis itself, despite its focus upon emotional categories, is driven by a desire to move beyond the emotional so that it can describe and explain reality more accurately. The psychoanalytical attitude seeks the patterns and structures of the empirically existing but otherwise inchoately experienced effects we regularly witness as a normal part of our everyday, lived environment. Both Freud and Lacan highlight how nominally empirical methods are innately unable to deal with those undeniably existing phenomena that we intuitively already know about but that evade conventional (social) scientific measurement. Keeping with the theme of dumplings, this distinction is demonstrated in medical research about the US obesity epidemic and the contradictory phenomenon of the French Paradox (France has less of an obesity problem than America, despite having a national diet rich in saturated fats). Empirical researchers concluded that a significant causal factor in US obesity is the larger average plate – and, by extension, portion – size compared to countries like France (see Wansink and Cheney 2005). Thus, whereas psychoanalysis tells us something we already knew at some level but are nonetheless surprised to reflect upon explicitly, excessively empirical thought is hidebound by the rigour of its methodology. It risks telling us something that we not only already knew explicitly, but are also unsurprised to be reminded about – in this case, the less-than-shocking conclusion that the disproportionately high level of American obesity is caused by Americans, on average . . . eating too much.

An apocryphal story relates how a cop finds a drunk under a street-light looking for his car keys that he dropped on the opposite, dark side of the street. When the cop asks why the drunk is looking for the keys in the wrong place, he receives the defensive retort: 'Because this is where the light is.' The drunk can be seen as emblematic of those analysts of the media for whom the light of methodological rigour is more important than the admittedly dark areas of the situation that nonetheless contain the keys to clearer insight. Additionally, the cop can be viewed as representing the psychoanalyst who questions the wisdom of ignoring where the keys actually lie because of the relative difficulty of the searching process beyond the light. The drunk's truculence also mirrors the resistance frequently displayed to psychoanalysis as so acerbically encapsulated in Karl Kraus's comment that '[p]sychoanalysis is the disease of which it claims to be the cure' (cited in Szaz 1990: 24). There is, however, also the contrasting danger, particularly relevant to Žižek the academic celebrity, of idealizing the seductive analyst who seems to have all the answers. In either case, '[w]hether the analyst is blamed or idealized, the result is the same: the neurosis is protected against the encroachment of analysis' (Thompson 1994: 184). Mindful of both positive and negative resistances to psychoanalytical insight, this book shows that it still (like a famous beer familiar to the drunk under the street-light) tends to refresh the parts that other methods cannot. Emotional reactions to Žižek's highbrow interrogation of popular low culture represent an unwillingness to deal with the basic, traumatic nature of the knowledge that results. Žižek's radical *materialist theology* is based upon facing up to the fact that 'reality' needs confronting without recourse to false abstraction *and simultaneously* recognizing that a key aspect of reality is its non-material, but no less powerful, libidinal impulses and drives.

MEDIA PSYCHOSIS AND NEUROSIS: THE UNKNOWN KNOWNS

While the commemorative ambivalences of neurosis are linked and limited to literature, literacy, and the printing press – and to their visualizable extensions, photography and film – only the psychotic witnesses the media-techno-logical institutions of 'liveness.' And although perversion may be the developed image of a negative associated with neurosis, its link to psychosis is conveyed via the mass media analogues specific to group psychology which turn on this 'live' transmission and broadcast – and turn around into devices of surveillance. (Rickels 1990: 50)

He's loved of the distracted multitude,
Who like not in their judgement, but their eyes.
(*Hamlet*, Act IV, Sc. iv)

The diagnostic approach of psychoanalysis relies upon the identification of symptomatic acts which Freud defines as 'those acts which people perform, as we say, automatically, unconsciously, without attending to them, or as in a moment of distraction' (Freud 2001c [1901–5]: 76). Significantly, in his seminal paper on the cultural impact of the earliest media technologies, 'Das Kunstwerk im Zeitalter seiner technischen Reproduzierbarkeit' ('The Work of Art in the Age of Mechanical Reproduction'), Walter Benjamin (1936) also identifies the deceptively simple term *distraction* (*zerstreuung*) as the key mode of receptivity in which people experience media technologies. More than the relatively superficial and vague term 'distraction', however, psychoanalysis enables us to address two deeper media symptoms: neurosis and psychosis. In Freud's terms: '. . . neurosis does not disavow the reality; it only ignores it; psychosis disavows it and tries to replace it' (Freud 2001f [1923–5]: 185). The modern mediascape is a manifold of these psychological conditions. Its various formats disavow and ignore reality in subtly conflated ways, as indicated by Rickels's above association between psychosis and technological mediation. Media spectacles embody layered belief structures explored throughout this book. In one sense we know that they are 'only' spectacles. In another sense, in many ways we act as if they are real and we only pretend to pretend to believe that they are mere representations – despite what we might say, in terms of actual doing, we treat them as if they were real.

According to Freud, a defining feature of neurotics is their failure to reach a workable accommodation between the competing pulls of reality and fantasy that constitute an inescapable feature of the human condition. This occurs to the extent that '[i]f what they long for the most intensely in their phantasies is presented to them in reality, they none the less flee from it; and they abandon themselves to their phantasies the most readily where they need no longer fear to see them realized' (Freud 2001c [1901–5]: 110). For Žižek, psychoanalysis is a form of understanding significant not just for individuals but for the mediascape at large. For example, from a Žižekian perspective, the US Government's post 9/11 declaration of war upon an abstract noun (the War on Terror) constituted a blend of acting out and *passage à l'acte*[3] – symptomatic of the world's most militarily powerful nation's inability to confront its own neurotic relationship with reality and its representations:

> . . . an act proper is . . . the very opposite of the violent *passage a l'acte*. What is a *passage à l'acte*? Perhaps, its ultimate cinematic expression is found in Paul Schrader's and Martin Scorsese's *Taxi Driver*, in the final outburst of Travis (Robert de Niro) against the pimps who control the young girl he wants to save (Jodie Foster). Crucial is the implicit suicidal dimension of this *passage à l'acte*: when Travis prepares for his attack he practices in front of the mirror the drawing of the gun; in what is the best-known scene of the film, he addresses his own image in the mirror with the aggressive-condescending 'You talkin' to me?' In a textbook illustration of Lacan's notion of the 'mirror stage,' aggressivity is here clearly aimed at oneself, at one's own mirror-image. This suicidal dimension reemerges at the end of the slaughter scene when Travis, heavily wounded and leaning at the wall, mimics with the fore-finger of his right hand a gun aimed at his blood-stained forehead and mockingly triggers it, as if saying 'The true aim of my outburst was myself.' (Žižek 2005a website)

The society-wide development of this neurosis was presciently described forty years before the tragic events of 9/11 in Daniel Boorstin's *The Image*:

> Of all nations in the world, the United States was built in nobody's image. It was the land of the unexpected, of unbounded hope, of ideals, of quest for an unknown perfection. It is all the more unfitting that we should offer ourselves in images. And all the more fitting that the images which we make wittingly or unwittingly to sell America to

the world should come back to haunt and curse us. (Boorstin 1992 [1961]: 245–6)

Žižek identified a basic choice that faced Americans at the historical juncture of 9/11. They could decide to retreat yet further into their already self-enclosed sphere of fantasy, 'leading to more aggressivity towards the threatening Outside, in short: to a paranoiac acting out. Or America will finally risk stepping through the fantasmatic screen separating it from the Outside World, accepting its arrival into the Real world' (*Desert*: 49). The media's response to the post 9/11 invasion of Iraq suggests that America has not stepped through the fantasmatic screen. Hyperrealist TV dramas such as *Over There* and *Generation Kill*, and movies like *Green Zone* and *The Hurt Locker*, depict in explicit detail the cheapness of Iraqi civilian life, viewed by US troops as a permanently threatening Other. The TV programmes in particular can be interpreted as part of a media-sponsored neurotic flight from reality-on-the-ground through the sublimation of war atrocities into entertainment; as Guy Debord expresses it: '. . . history itself haunts modern society like a spectre, pseudo-histories are constructed at every level of consumption of life in order to preserve the threatened equilibrium of present frozen time' (Debord 1977 [1967]: N200).

The media's role in the psychotic reconstruction of an alternate reality in which the Outside is targeted for paranoiac destruction can be seen in the recent WikiLeaks publication of classified US military video footage taken from an Apache helicopter (see Collateral Murder 2010) that was used to attack and machine-gun to death a group of Iraqi civilians, two of whom were Reuters journalists. Subsequent to the initial shooting, an Iraqi civilian van with two small children in the front seat arrived on the scene to pick up the dead and wounded and was also fired upon. The following soldiers' transcript comes from the immediate aftermath of both shooting incidents:

> 04:31 Oh, yeah, look at those dead bastards.
> 04:36 Nice.
> 04:37 Two-Six; Crazyhorse One-Eight.
> 04:44 Nice.
> . . .
> 16:49 Roger, I've got uh eleven Iraqi KIAs [Killed In Action]. One small child wounded. Over.
> 16:57 Roger. Ah damn. Oh well.
> 17:04 Roger, we need, we need a uh to evac [evacuate] this child. Ah, she's got a uh, she's got a wound to the belly.
> . . .
> 17:46 Well it's their fault for bringing their kids into a battle.
> 17:48 That's right.

This short excerpt portrays a segue from the psychotic enjoyment of killing to neurotic flight from the reality of accepting moral responsibility for one's actions. The wounding of a child is superficially acknowledged but immediately an attempt is made to avoid facing up to that reality: 'Well it's their fault for bringing their kids into a battle.' The problem for Western viewers of this video footage is that whilst they may be able to disassociate themselves from the soldiers' psychosis, it is less easy to achieve similar distance from the pervasive neurosis of a society of the spectacle in which these images, undeniably raw, are nevertheless soon integrated and contained. Dominated by our eyes and not our judgement, as a distracted multitude, initial acknowledgement of mediated psychosis soon dissipates. Debord wrote: 'In a world which *really is topsy-turvy*, the true is a moment of the false' (Debord 1977 [1967]: N9). Thus, the truly traumatic *Collateral Murder* footage is indicative of, and contributes to, a culture that is able to co-opt such trauma into TV shows, movies, and, perhaps most disconcertingly, 'interactive' computer games like *Battlefield: Bad Company* and *Six Days Fallujah*. In Žižek's analysis, media *causes célèbres* are delusive. Their apparent exceptionality disguises how the sense of unease they produce comes from the way we are reminded of something we already know but neurotically tend to avoid admitting to ourselves. Hence, an under-acknowledged feature of the infamous Abu Ghraib photographs was how '[t]o anyone acquainted with the American way of life, the photographs brought to mind the obscene underside of US popular culture' (Žižek 2004a website). Žižek argues that the pictures resonated with high school and military hazing incidents frequently reported in the US press. To underline his point, he quotes Donald Rumsfeld's now 'well-known' comments:

'There are known knowns. These are things we know that we know. There are known unknowns. That is to say, there are things that we know we don't know. But there are also unknown unknowns. There are things we don't know we don't know.' What he forgot to add was the crucial fourth term: the 'unknown knowns,' the things we don't know that we know – which is precisely, the Freudian unconscious, the 'knowledge which doesn't know itself,' as Lacan used to say.

If Rumsfeld thinks that the main dangers in this confrontation with Iraq were the 'unknown unknowns,' that is, the threats from Saddam whose nature we cannot even suspect, then the Abu Ghraib scandal shows that the main dangers lie in the 'unknown knowns' – the disavowed beliefs, suppositions and obscene practices we pretend not to know about, even though they form the background of our public values. (Žižek 2004a website)

Inspired by Rumsfeld, it is these *unknown knowns* that Žižek uncovers in his analysis of the media, which expands upon Debord's concise definition of the spectacle as 'the concrete inversion of life ... the autonomous movement of the non-living' (Debord 1977 [1967]: N2). Paraphrasing Shakespeare and Marx, in a contemporary society of the spectacle that contains such daily cast of brazen cannon as the Nike advertisement in which Tiger Woods listens to his dead father (albeit an Earl not a king), the spectres harrowing us with entertainment and wonder are those capitalist forms of 'non-life' in which the accumulation of dead labour converted into images comes to haunt the living with commercial stalk. 'Tis not but our fantasy, nor a mote to trouble the mind's eye, but a portentous figure that vividly encapsulates how, coming out of the Woods today, the unknown knowns of the *Just Do It* ethos manifest themselves, since the public relations' play is the Thing.

GETTING A TIGER OUT OF THE WOODS

... psychoanalysts 'seem to take to Hamlet like kittens to a ball of yarn.' (Holland cited in Muller 1980: 147)

[Ophelia] provides an essential pivot in the hero's progress toward his mortal rendezvous with his act – an act that he carries out, in some sense, in spite of himself. There is a level in the subject on which it can be said that his fate is expressed in terms of a pure signifier, a level at which he is merely the reverse-side of a message that is not even his own. (Lacan et al. 1977: 12)

Wednesday, 7 April 2010, saw the first TV airing of an artfully filmed black and white advertisement by Nike in which Tiger Woods, in head shot, face impassive, listens to the voice of his dead father. Tiger stands in appropriately wooden fashion – a silent monument to the limitations of *Just Do It*, but, as with the sublime objects of ideology to be encountered throughout this book, he belatedly does nothing so that we can continue to 'just do it'. Confronted by Tiger Woods' all too enthusiastic commitment to just doing it, the castration complacency complex (see below) extends its reach to even beyond the grave as Tiger and the audience hear the voice of his dead father. As Leo Lowenthal pointed out: 'Mass culture is psychoanalysis in reverse' (cited in Jay 1996 [1973]: 173), and thus, evoking the role of the psychoanalyst, Earl Woods says, 'Tiger, I am more prone to be inquisitive to promote discussion. I want to find out what your thinking was. I want to find out what your feelings are, and did you learn anything?' Conscious of Holland's quip about kittens, it is nevertheless too tempting not to find resonance between this advertisement and Lacan's above interpretation of the situation Hamlet encounters.

According to Lacan, Hamlet acts 'in spite of himself' and 'his fate is expressed in terms of a pure signifier ... the reverse-side of a message that is not even his own'. Both Hamlet and Tiger Woods find themselves acting in a play within a play – *le massage à l'acte* in which Hamlet seeks to confirm his step-father's guilt through a mouse trap whilst Nike use a chiaroscuro play of public relations to evade a honey trap (prurient media reports of a golf player playing away from home). A crucial difference, however, is that whilst Hamlet has to take revenge for his step-father's concupiscence, in Nike's adaptation, the ghost of Earl Woods intones so that his son may atone for his own much-publicized sins. Hamlet is often treated as almost synonymous with the notion of procrastination, so we tend to forget the number of times in the play in which he acts extremely rashly – the killing of Polonius being a prime example. On the key question of revenging his father, filled with tortuous self-doubt, he questions the cause for his own lack of action: '. . . whether it be / Bestial oblivion, or some craven scruple / Of thinking too precisely on the event' (Act IV, Sc. iv) that prevents him from just doing it. By contrast, in Nike's case, a craven corporate scruple of thinking precisely on the public relations event is applied to compensate for rash acts of bestial oblivion already committed.

Tiger Woods is obviously a particularly high-profile example of the way in which the actions and self-identity of individuals are filtered through the medium of society. To convey the psychoanalytical notion of the big Other (see Chapter 3), which describes the immaterial but deeply influential repository of ideas and values that structures society, Žižek rhetorically asks:

> What is symbolic efficiency? We all know the old, worn-out joke about a madman who thought he was a grain of corn; after being finally cured and sent home, he immediately returned to the mental institution, explaining to the doctor his panic: 'On the road, I encountered a hen, and I was afraid it would eat me!' To the doctor's surprised exclamation, 'But what's the problem now? You know you're not a grain but a man who cannot be swallowed by a hen!', the madman answered 'Yes, I know I am no longer a grain, but does the hen know it?' (Žižek 1997a website)

Lacan distinguishes between the traditional hero, like Oedipus, whose tragedy is that he acts in ignorance (or in the case of Othello an ignorance compounded by his jealous predisposition), and the modern hero, like Hamlet, whose tragedy stems from knowing that one's acts may have drastic consequences for oneself and others. Rather than being hamstrung through ignorance, Hamlet's difficulties stem from what to do with prior knowledge: 'The person who knows is indeed in such a perilous position, marked for failure and sacrifice, that he is led to feign madness, and even, as Pascal says, to be mad along with everyone else. Feigning madness is thus one of the dimensions of what we might call the strategy of the modern hero' (Lacan et al. 1977: 20). Developing Lacan's schema further, figures like Tiger Woods illustrate the most recent form of the postmodern media hero who, like the audience, feigns a socially sanctioned madness. This is the contemporary form of ideology emphasized repeatedly by Žižek, a form in which we all claim to know better but still act as if we don't – we pretend to pretend to believe so that the ultimate outcome is a mediascape suffused with a naturalized form of bad faith. In a Rumsfeldian twist, we are reduced to participating in a media environment in which it is not the case that the chicken knows or doesn't know, but rather, one in which the chicken knows we know that he knows that we know. What makes Žižek's combination of psychoanalytical and philosophical method so useful for revealing the true nature of the media's mode of operation is his strong commitment to the truth, but the full nature of truth as it appears today in all its relational heavily mediated intricacy.

MEDIA *DURCHARBEITUNG* AND THE TROUBLE WITH DORA

I have a hat, but I do not have a rabbit. (Žižek in Bowman and Stamp 2007: xvi)

Freud's thoughts about transference contained an elasticity that is easily lost on the literal-minded. (Thompson 1994: 193)

As Thompson points out, a standard overly literal mis-
interpretation of the psychoanalytical method confuses
the empirical validity of what is said during an analytical
encounter with the deeper truth that comes *through* the analytical process. Sharing a similar approach to the joke-work
and dream-work of psychoanalysis, Žižek's media analysis
succeeds where others fail in addressing the contemporary
conveyance of ideological *effect via form*. In addition to the
fundamental rule of absolute candour (to the analyst as
Other, but most importantly oneself), the analytic attitude
requires what Freud called *Durcharbeitung* – 'working-
through'. This effort is required because, as we will see a
number of times in the following pages, knowledge of our
various forms of resistance to the truth is not enough (*je sais
bien mais quand-même . . .*); we also need to learn to own and
become fully conversant with our modes of resistance if we
ever aim to either overcome them, or at least reach a responsible accommodation with their intractable existence. The
problem with the various sublime objects and processes of
ideology described in the subsequent chapters is that they
assume on our behalf, so that we are excused from working-
through and taking responsibility for the psychopathology
of our everyday mediated lives. Media theorists resistant to
the working-through that Žižek provides thereby revive the
example of Dora, Freud's first major case history. Rather
than invest in the required *Durcharbeitung*, she continued
for the rest of her life to prefer her neurotically disproportionate investment in fantasy over a painful, but necessary,
encounter with fantasy's vexed relationship with reality.

For some critics, Žižek's concentration upon the ideological role played by fantasy at the expense of concrete
solutions is unacceptable irrespective of the accuracy of the
analysis. Thus, summarizing Žižek's critical account of the
contemporary media's *plague of fantasies* and responding to

Žižek's statement that he has a hat but no rabbit, Critchley argues:

> Reality is structured by belief, by a faith in fantasy that we know to be fantasy yet we believe nonetheless. This is a stunning diagnostic insight, yet my question is and always has been: what does one *do* with this insight? . . . My question is: where is the rabbit? We need at least one rabbit, maybe more if we want them to breed. (Critchley in Bowman and Stamp 2007: xv and xvi)

Here, Critchley commits the theoretical equivalent of censuring the medieval apothecary for identifying a case of the bubonic plague because he cannot then provide an immediate cure. Limited as Žižek's practical solutions might be, his recognition of the constitutive power of fantasy is paradoxically more realistic than much more sober but politically Panglossian diagnoses; as Žižek argues: 'What is needed is a concrete analysis of the rabbits breeding around, not cheap rhetorics on how it is better to have a rabbit than not to have it' (ibid.: 204). Like the psychoanalytical method he draws upon, Žižek's media analysis introduces a much needed element of temporality to the mediascape's pervasively insistent simultaneity. Whilst capitalist media privileges 'reality-based' formats because of their rabbit-like ability to reproduce themselves, Žižek encourages us to step back and, rather than chase after the rabbits, consider the out-of-control breeding as the real problem. He counsels against the false consolations of pseudo-activity that creates a misleading impression of political progress – a Nike-like 'just do it' cod-philosophical marketing campaign that sums up a social mentality that has reached far beyond the consumption of sports goods to complacently castrate the testicles from the body politic.

CASTRATION COMPLACENCY COMPLEX: A SYMBOLLOCKALLY PERVERTED TALE OF TWO POLITICAL PARTIES

Tony Blair's attack dog Alastair sniffed the air and smelled a scandal. He who routinely dismissed unwelcome news stories as 'bollocks', 'complete bollocks' and 'bollocks on stilts'. (Danchev 2005: 247)

In psychoanalytical theory, *castration* is a technical concept that refers to the inevitable loss that accompanies humanity's entry into the symbolic order. Language allows us to describe reality whilst simultaneously, and *by the very act of communication*, distancing us from direct experience of raw reality. For example, the word 'tree' allows us to usefully talk about all trees but, at the same time, a sense of the uniqueness of each individual tree is now lost (castrated) by our use of the generic term. We obviously gain a great deal when we enter the symbolic order, but we also sacrifice something. In terms of the media, the extent of this loss and its manipulated cover-up is frequently underestimated. For example, during the UK's 1997 General Election campaign, as Director of Communications for the British political party 'New' Labour (formerly a traditionally socialist party known rather more plainly as 'Labour'), Peter Mandelson provided an interesting political spin on castration. He received focus group feedback that New Labour was perceived as poor at safeguarding Britain's independence from the political depredations of the European Union. In response,

Mandelson pressed on with unveiling, on his own terms, his secret weapon: his cherished party election broadcast with 'Fitz' the bulldog to underline the robust Britishness of the campaign. He was fastidious about it in only one respect.

A note from the ad agency BMP warned that the dog's testicles were just visible in the shadow; should they be airbrushed out? 'Yes please,' Mandelson wrote in the margin. It was, as Mandelson would remark later, to be a 'very New Labour dog'. (Macintyre 1999)

Unlike the genuinely felt emotion of Jesse Jackson's reference to castration when he was overheard in a TV studio saying of President Obama 'I want to cut his nuts off' (CNN 2008), and Alastair Campbell's above alleged facility with testicular language, Mandelson's mode of castration was designed to avoid any unwelcome reminders of an earthy reality that might muddy his seamlessly mediated political advertisement – the awkward presence of the dog's testicles at the dinner/political party: 'So that was Mandelson's idea of what the Labour party should be. A proud and patriotic beast but with no bollocks' (O'Farrell 2001).

Theodor Adorno, the Frankfurt School critical theorist, memorably argued that whilst true 'works of art are ascetic and unashamed; the culture industry is pornographic and prudish' (Adorno 2001: 10). In other words, contemporary culture can be comfortably explicit about such easily representable things as sex but conversely squeamish about more intractably ambiguous and ultimately unrepresentable aspects of the human condition: for example, the full implications and responsibilities that accompany a loving relationship, of which sexuality forms but one part. Mandelson provided a political twist to the 'pornographic' element of Adorno's aphorism. In the role of the Secretary of State for Business, Innovation and Skills (in practice, second only to the Prime Minister in terms of political power), he revealed how prudishness about the dog's testicles can indeed coincide with a corresponding facility with pornographic expression. Angered by an announcement by the News International

corporation's *Sun* UK tabloid newspaper that it had decided
to withdraw its support from New Labour, Mandelson was
allegedly overheard calling executives from the corporation 'cunts'. When questioned by the press, Mandelson
admitted he had used a c-word, but that the word had been
'chumps' – a semantic bowdlerization of female genitalia to
match his previous semiotic manipulation of unwanted testicles (see Channel 4 News 2009; Guardian Mediamonkey
2009; Pickard 2009). In British politics, Mandelson acted
as the official, emollient face of ideology-in-action, so that
being caught out using a shocking expression represented
a rare loss of media control, although one that was quickly
and masterfully corrected. By contrast, Alastair Campbell,
his successor as New Labour's Director of Communications,
directly embodied the obscene underside to airbrushed New
Labour. Widely considered to be the model for the fictional
character Malcom Tucker, the foul-mouthed Scottish press
secretary from the British TV satire *The Thick of It* (Amando
Ianucci 2005) and subsequent Hollywood movie *In The Loop*
(Amando Ianucci 2009), Campbell, with his infamously col-
ourful language, illustrated Žižek's notion that an obscene
underside is not an accidental by-product of a power structure but its direct corollary. Campbell's particular form
of testicular crudities (see above quotation) reacquaints,
if only metaphorically, the p/Party's dog with the genitals
Mandelson was so keen to remove from view.

The disproportionate amount of airtime and column
inches the media devoted to Mandelson's ingenious denial
of his alleged Anglo-Saxon profanity distracts us from much
more significantly obscene political acts. Unlike the foolish
peasant's deluded notion of literally having power 'by the
balls', Mandelson's cynically knavish airbrushing marked
the early stages of his on-going emasculation of a whole
political party – his very real and painful castration of the

traditionally socialist Labour Party and its re-branding as market-friendly, soap-powder-sounding New Labour. The re-launch included the adoption of a red rose for the new party's logo, a reassuringly floral domestication of the colour red's 'unfortunate' historical association with political movements that have been open about their desire to tackle capital's power at its source. Lacan points out that an important element of the knave's ideological mode of operating is the way in which he presents himself: '. . . to play the role of what he is in fact, namely, a "knave". In other words, he doesn't retreat from the consequences of what is called realism; that is, when required he admits he's a crook' (Lacan cited in *Plague*: 45). The increased interpretative sophistication of media audiences, however, requires an updating of Lacan's insight. Now the form in which the conservative knave owns up to his guilt is more complicated. It is no longer simply a case of our admiration for the openness of an admission of guilt, or the convincing nature of any outright denial, but rather, with examples like Mandelson's use of 'chumps', we now admire the skilful attenuation of the obvious – the contemporary media's *castration complacency*. In this particular case, Mandelson's knavish skills of 'symbollock' media manipulation are enjoyed at the cost of ever greater distance from the political substance for which the Labour Party was originally founded.

The fittingly seminal moment that symbolized the end of the New Labour project occurred due to a momentary irruption of true feeling into the complacency complex. Hoisted by his own microphone, after a walk-about designed for the TV cameras during the final stages of the 2010 UK General Election campaign, the soon-to-be defeated incumbent Prime Minister, Gordon Brown, was heard insulting a plain-speaking voter. Shortly after a slightly testy but essentially civil conversation with Gillian Duffy, an elderly lifelong

Labour voter, on getting back into his car Brown was caught referring to Mrs Duffy as a 'bigoted woman'. Immediately and predictably referred to by the Press as 'Bigotgate', the incident portrayed New Labour as having lost its hitherto almost preternatural ability to contain non-mediated irritants through the expert manipulation of its genuinely held prejudice against the genuinely held convictions of others. The impact of the gaffe was heightened when Brown was later filmed in a BBC radio studio hearing a recording of his words being played out on the national airwaves. Brown sat slumped with his head in his hands, or, as the American political satirist Jon Stewart expressed it: 'You can actually see the moment when his political career leaves his body' (*The Daily Show*, Thursday, 29 April 2010).

CONCLUSION: CRITICAL ELASTRATION AND THE PHILOSOPHER'S STONES

... critical Leftists have hitherto only succeeded in soiling those in power, whereas the real point is to castrate them. ... The task is not to conduct the castration in a direct climactic confrontation, but to undermine those in power with patient ideologico-critical work, so that although they are still in power, one all of a sudden notices that the powers-that-be are afflicted with unnaturally high voices. (*Tragedy*: 7)

In a theoretically perverted response to the media manipulations carried out by the powerful, Žižek suggests a radically orientated form of castration akin to the elastrator method in which a ram's scrotum is banded with rings until it slowly atrophies away. Žižek's unapologetic privileging of theory is a much-needed response to the on-going castration of not just critical thought, but any thought premised upon non-corporate values. In this regard, the UK's recent experience is instructive. Previously and unsurprisingly contained within the Department of Education, in the then renamed Department for Innovation, Universities, and Skills the university sector was still explicitly recognized (if commercially sandwiched). Subsequently, it was completely cut off as universities were subsumed within the even more commercially explicit unit run by Mandelson – the Department for Business, Innovation, and Skills (see Taylor 2008a and 2010). Žižek's popularity can be seen as a countervailing reaction to the manner by which 'the university is designed to ensure that thought never has any repercussions' (Lacan 2008: 26). His work answers Hannah Arendt's call (after Kant) for an 'enlarged mentality', 'training the imagination to go visiting' (Arendt 1982: 43) and 'thinking without a banister' (Hill 1979: 334). Žižek's first-hand experience of Communist life in the former Yugoslavia has provided him with a valuable sensitivity to the ways in which the West's much-vaunted freedoms are frequently squandered in a climate of training for training's sake, thinking with a stair-lift, and etiolated thought.

Žižek draws attention to the significance of the title of the Lacanian school's early periodical *Silicet* (literally 'it is permitted to know'), when it is contrasted with *videlicet* ('it is permitted to see'), which characterizes the dominant mindset within liberal democracies. His crucial point is that 'the very fascination with the obscenity we are allowed to observe prevents us from *knowing what it is that we see*' (*Tragedy*: 8). Thus, to paraphrase Adorno's previously quoted phrase, the superficially pornographic nature of today's mediascape distracts us from its compensatory prudishness in other areas of social life. Lacan humorously observed that '[i]f you open them, psychoanalytical journals are the chastest things in the world. They no longer tell stories about fucking. They leave that to the dailies' (Lacan 2008: 19). A great part of Žižek's value lies in the way in which he has responded to this situation in which the shocking, revelatory power of theory has largely been colonized by the mass media's overwhelmingly explicit presence in our lives. In Žižek's hands, media content is not left alone and his theory is definitely not chaste – it unashamedly demonstrates that although undoubtedly often obscene, the low-brow detritus of traditional folk stories and mass media culture embody very accessible representations of otherwise off-puttingly esoteric theoretical issues. Excessive sensitivity to Žižek's deliberate use of surface-level obscenity overlooks the much greater obscenity he is highlighting: the destructive features of our cultural and economic systems that we routinely fail (or refuse) to register. Since the repressed always returns, these unacknowledged features reappear as symptoms waiting to be detected in jokes, anecdotes, and, most significantly for our purposes, media content.

Lying behind Žižek's *épater le bourgeois* tendencies and vulgar humour is thus a deadly serious critique of the contemporary media's ideological impact. The punchline twists and surface-level obscenity of such provocative examples as his detailed consideration of the UK's first 'masturbate-a-thon' (*Violence*: 25–30) serve profound political and philosophical ends. Instead of Žižek's provocations offending us all too readily, they should remind us of the dangers that otherwise lurk beneath the surface-level decorum of the socially acceptable. Much can be learnt from the consequences of the acquiescent behaviour of the anti-Nazi German officer Field Marshal von Kluge, who, although willing to help assassinate Hitler, nevertheless vetoed an otherwise viable plot planned by a group of officers scheduled to eat with Hitler because 'it is not seemly to shoot a man at lunch' (cited in *Lost Causes*: 18). Žižek points out how, '[i]n his *German Ideology*, Marx mockingly observes that philosophy relates to "actual life" as masturbation to the sexual act' (*Tarrying*: 3). Whilst some of his fiercest critics may similarly dismiss Žižek as a philosophical wanker whose work is a load of bollocks, admirers and detractors alike must admit that, whatever else can be said, unlike Field Marshal von Kluge, Mandelson's New Labour, and assorted quisling apologists for the media's worst excesses, but like Fitz the bulldog, Žižek's perverse theory certainly has balls.

2

ŽIŽEK'S TICKLING SHTICK

INTRODUCTION: THE PHILOSOPHICAL SERIOUSNESS OF DIONYSIAN JOKES

Jokes have not received nearly as much philosophical consideration as they deserve in view of the part they play in our mental life. (Freud 2001d [1905]: 9)

Phallic songs were sung during rituals honoring Dionysus. In these rituals the participants would march in procession, carrying a phallus of huge proportions made of animal skins, and singing obscene songs, full of ambiguous innuendo. (Zupančič 2008: 213)

The previous chapter explored how Žižek's inimitable brand of theoretical perversity gains him notoriety and media attention but also creates the risk that his substantive intellectual points are lost amidst either the sparks of his short-circuits or po-faced annoyance at his use of filthy humour and/or speculative psychoanalytical insights – as Freud noted: 'Only jokes that have a purpose run the risk of meeting with people who do not want to listen to them' (Freud 2001d [1905]: 90). This chapter further develops the conceptual significance of Žižek's pervertedly humorous analysis by unpacking in more detail how it acts as a particularly well-calibrated tool for understanding the mediascape's imbrication of fantasy and reality. Freud highlights the efficiency with which jokes draw attention to the intertwined nature of form and content within the act of communication. Meta-reflexively using a joke to marry form and content whilst simultaneously discussing form's relationship to content, he endorses the notion that jokes are a powerful force for uncovering the hidden aspects of situations through their provocative juxtaposition of otherwise dissimilar things. He relates how: 'Jean Paul has expressed this thought itself in a joking form: "Joking is the disguised priest who weds every couple." Vischer . . . carries this further: "He likes best to wed couples whose union their relatives frown upon"' (ibid.: 11). It is perhaps unsurprising therefore that, as a high priest of theory who regularly marries mass media to philosophy, Žižek's work often meets with frowning disapproval.

The Ticklish Subject is sub-titled *The Absent Centre of Political Ontology*, pointing to the manifold issues that lie behind the superficially simple notion of ticklishness. The psychoanalyst Adam Phillips alludes to these deeper connotations of the tickle: 'The word speaks of the precarious, and so of the erotic. To tickle is, above all, to seduce, often by amusement' (Phillips 1994: 2). The richer, metaphorical sense of tickling thus goes beyond the merely physical act and the apparently innocent enjoyment of a 'childish' tickle. It relates to some of the frequently underestimated aspects of theory and the very serious purposes to which Žižek applies both humour and perversion. The seemingly unproblematic and self-explanatory scenario of a child's unalloyed enjoyment of being tickled is actually a nuanced, psychologically multi-layered experience because that 'child, in the ordinary, affectionate, perverse scenario of being tickled, is wholly exploitable' (ibid.: 1–2). This contradictory conflation of the 'ordinary, affectionate', and 'perverse' is what the deceptively simple tickle so seamlessly enacts. For Phillips, far from an epitome of childish innocence, the tickle is part of an 'elaborate repertoire of intrusions' (ibid.: 3) through which a child learns about the nature of its relations to adult figures of authority. By extension, the inherently ambiguous nature of tickling provides a good example of Žižek's psychoanalytically informed analysis of the similar ambiguities that structure our ticklishly mediated adult lives.

Translated into English as *Jokes and Their Relation to the Unconscious* (1905), the original German title of Freud's work, *Der Witz und seine Beziehung zum Unbewußten*, is more allusive. *Der Witz* relates to both mental ability and the product of that ability – wittiness, use of the witticism, and, more generally still, 'ingenuity' (see Strachey in ibid.: 7). Perverted jokes are particularly useful for Žižek's ingeniously witty approach to the media because, in their very mode of functioning, they bring forward hysterical knowledge (generally from an otherwise everyday situation) that would otherwise remain concealed and hidden (or at least unremarked upon). Jokes achieve this effect in a manner that mirrors the way in which media ideology works – the seamless conflation of form and content, the wheelbarrow that gets by the security guard, or, as McLuhan describes how the medium becomes the message: '. . . the "content" of a medium is like the juicy piece of meat carried by the burglar to distract the watchdog of the mind' (McLuhan 1995 [1964]: 32). With the exception of slapstick's derivation of humour from excessive physicality, 'the joke resides in the expression which the thought has been given in the sentence' (Freud 2001d [1905]: 16). This intertwining of form and content occurs in a highly naturalized, subconscious manner. Because of its humorous effect, the ideological significance of the psychological process involved in the joke-work tends to be overlooked. Like media ideology's paradoxically open form of deception (the stolen wheelbarrow), when faced with a joke, '[w]e grant it logical or practical consequences in excess of its true content, only to deny these consequences as soon as we have clearly recognized the nature of the remark' (Lipps cited in ibid.: 12). Put another way, whether it is in the hands of a good politician, film director, or, as we shall now see, a comedian, the basic process that underlies ideology reinforces the subtlety of its impact through an in-built quality of plausible deniability – the 'ambiguous innuendo' that Zupančič describes above in its early historical context.

The now octogenarian UK comedian Ken Dodd provides an interesting embodiment of the symbolic order's ticklish mix of contradictory elements – the ordinary yet perverse, the affectionate and exploitable. Famous for his 'tickling stick' – a large feather duster that draws upon the phallic symbolism of the ancient Dionysian tradition – Dodd seduces the audience by the humour obtained from the stick's status as both innocent and perverse. In turn, his general mode of humour (shtick) exploits the affectionate and ordinary relationship he has with his audience, the better to convey abnormal meaning. With songs like 'That's the Wrong Way to Tickle Mary', the effect is obvious, but, irrespective of authorial intention, it can also be perceived in the seemingly *über*-ordinary but endowment-allusive song 'Happiness'. Typically waving his tickling stick, Dodd sings the homophonically suggestive titular lyric twice for emphasis, proclaiming it is 'the greatest thing that I possess' and thanking the Lord for blessing him 'with more than my share of happiness'.[1] In other areas of Dodd's repertoire, the various ticklish elements identified by Phillips – intrusion, fantasy, humour, and perversity – all come together in a less implied phallic fashion as in the evocative joke: 'What a beautiful day for sticking a cucumber through the vicar's letterbox and shouting "the Martians are coming!"' Dodd's trademark *double-entendres* represent in an emblematically comic form the media's much more matter-of-fact but deeply serious ideological modes of operation. Žižek enthusiastically engages with the symbolic order's ticklishly insubstantial but powerfully affective morass of desire, fantasy, drives, and superegoic injunctions that bombard us on a daily basis.

TICKLISH SUBJECTS: KINKY FEATHERS, *FORREST GUMP*, AND THE CHICKEN THAT DOES NOT KNOW

From the fact that a child can hardly tickle itself, or in a much less degree than when tickled by another person, it seems that the precise point to be touched must not be known. (Charles Darwin)[2]

If you tickle us do we not laugh? (Shylock – *The Merchant of Venice*, Act III, Sc. i)

How tickled I am! (Ken Dodd)

Although the propensity of readers to be tickled by 'a penis' in an otherwise perfectly innocent song about happiness will vary, people's differing sensitivity to literal and symbolic ticklishness is part of the social aspect of what is normally thought about solely as an individual physical idiosyncrasy. But before we can even begin to consider the manner in which a subject may be tickled, Žižek highlights the inescapable social context of what we might alternatively like to think of as an autonomous subject. A single subject only exists as such through *subject*(ion) to a surrounding symbolic order, and, far from neutral and 'normal', that symbolic order functions on the basis of ambiguous libidinal forces that the media *mediates*. In *Casablanca*, ideology's mode of operation can be seen in the scene towards the end of the film when Ilsa (Ingrid Bergman) visits Rick (Humphrey Bogart's) in order to obtain his help in obtaining transit letters so that she and her husband, Victor Laszlo, can escape. In desperation, Ilsa pulls a gun on Rick, quickly followed by a cathartic embrace during which she emotes: 'If you knew how much I loved you, how much I still love you,' then:

> The movie dissolves to 3 1/2 second shot of the airport tower at night, its searchlight circling, and then dissolves back to a shot from outside the window of Rick's room, where he is standing, looking out, and smoking a cigarette. . . . The question that immediately pops up here, of course, is: what happened in between, during the 3 1/2 second shot of the airport – did they DO IT or not? . . . what we encounter here is the clear example of the fetishistic split, of the disavowal-structure of '*je sais bien, mais quand même* . . .': the very awareness that they did not do it gives free rein to your dirty imagination – you can indulge in it, because you are absolved from the guilt by the fact that, for the big Other, they definitely did NOT do it . . . (Žižek 2007a website)

This exhibits the crucial contemporary ideological process the media plays by assuming the status of a big Other that legitimizes our attitude of *I know, but even so* – an attitude that pervades media audiences and which Lord Mandelson relied upon with his impressively dextrous use of the word 'chumps'.

Charles Darwin was correct in saying one cannot tickle oneself, but wrong in suggesting that the precise location of the tickling point is unknown. Most people do know where they are ticklish but, crucially, this knowledge is only useful when shared with one's tickler, or, by extension within the overarching symbolic order within which we find ourselves tickled in various non-physical ways. Phillips problematizes the apparently self-contained and exclusively physical nature of the tickle to rhetorically ask: '. . . what is the quality – that is to say, the fantasy – of the experience? . . . Is the tickling scene, at its most reassuring, not a unique representation of the overdisplacement of desire and, at its most unsettling, a paradigm of the perverse contract?' (Phillips 1994: 3). Prefiguring our later detailed exploration of Žižek's account of the ideological role of fantasy and the media's function as a vehicle for that role, Phillips's question about the relationship between tickling and perversion can be explored through the appropriate medium of a feather used by a happily married couple in order to spice up their sex life. Whilst a certain sense of mutual embarrassment may accompany their initial use of this new prop,

> no one is likely to dispute that they are creatively pursuing the joys of eroticism. Yet, if the same couple were to build sexual confidence as a result of their deeply satisfying experience with the added sensation and subsequently decide to exchange the feather for an entire bird, they might feel less embarrassed about the act, yet there is no doubt that it would be invariably perceived as perverse. Why is using a plumed feather for sexual purposes regarded as 'healthy', 'normal' and 'erotic', whereas employing a whole bird is unequivocally considered 'sick', 'bizarre', 'abnormal', 'deviant' and 'pathological'? When does the erotic become kinky? How far can our couple

extrapolate, quantitatively or qualitatively, on their single feather before entering the realm of perversion? And where shall we situate the bird's cut-off point? Where lies the object's boundary that separates the pleasurable play of normal eroticism from the painful pathology of abnormal perversion? A wing? A drumstick, perhaps? (Nobus 2006: 3)

The 'natural' response from most readers when faced with the above scenario is likely to be something along that lines of: 'A feather is fine, but a whole bird? That is *so* wrong!' However, identifying the exact grounds from which we draw our answer to this ticklish symbolic question is much more difficult than finding the precise location of a physical tickling spot.

A literal response to the question of the feather/whole bird spectrum of sexual perversion might be that a feather is objectively erotic because of the pleasurable sensory consequences of its delicate physical properties. Whilst correct, the deeper truth addressed by Žižek's psychoanalytical method is that, notwithstanding this literal observation, all sorts of misleadingly mundane objects and activities are liable to become enmeshed within our tortuously seething libidinal economies. For Freud, a perversion becomes a cause for analytical concern when it

is found to lie not in the *content* of the new sexual aim but in its relation to the normal. If a perversion, instead of appearing merely *alongside* the normal sexual aim and object . . . ousts them completely and takes their place in *all* circumstances – if, in short, a perversion has the characteristics of exclusiveness and fixation – then we shall usually be justified in regarding it as a pathological symptom. (Freud 2001c [1901–5]: 161)

The psychoanalytical conceptualization of perversion is thus highly useful for examining the mutually constitutive form/ content manner in which the media produces its effects – the feather-light ticklishness with which the medium becomes the massage. Our contemporary fixation with celebrity, for example, has become a pathological symptom that runs throughout the mediascape, now including formerly relatively insulated areas like political reporting. The erotic status of a couple's feather and the ideological status of media content both depend upon a relational position within an evolving symbolic order. As any viewer of the highly charged repartee between Cary Grant and Grace Kelly throughout Hitchcock's *To Catch A Thief* can testify, when Grace Kelly politely enquires during a picnic scene, 'Breast or leg?' sometimes a drumstick is much more than just a drumstick.

Moving on to a complete turkey, a controversy that resulted from George Bush's visit to US troops in Iraq for their 2003 Thanksgiving Dinner displays the perverse manner in which the media mediates symbolic communication. The controversy centred upon a photo-opportunity in which the President was shown in a mess tent carrying a large roasted turkey which was claimed to be plastic.[3] Initially, critics of George Bush made much mileage of this pseudo-event, comparing it to other photo-opportunities such as the (in)famous 'Mission Accomplished' press conference upon the US aircraft carrier USS *Lincoln* on 1 May 2003. It has since been argued that the turkey in question was in fact a real one, with the caveat that it was a 'trophy' bird, designed for display purposes only whilst the troops were actually served processed turkey meat on canteen trays. As in the case of the eroticized feather, an overly literal, denotative dispute over the exact nature of the turkey (was it real or plastic?) misses the ultimately much more significant issue of the connotative position the bird assumes. The immense figurative freight of the Thanksgiving holiday for the American people is the most obvious aspect of its place within the symbolic order, but that significance is further mediated by the bird's further position within the pseudo-event nature of the photo-opportunity that prompted President Bush to carry the turkey at all. In this sort of situation, psychoanalytically informed theory has a distinct comparative advantage over empirically fixated methods because its notion of perversion allows it to adopt a position of reflexive critical distance to the role played by fixation itself – the perversion here lies not in the plastic/real quality of the turkey, but the adaptation of Presidential behaviour solely to fit within the frame of a public relations photograph.

The big Other can have much greater significance than merely concerning the unfortunate hallucinations of a psychiatric patient who fears he is a grain of corn,[4] or the poultry-bearing activities of a president. It can play a crucial mediating role in the political experience of whole countries. For example, Žižek describes how in the last years of Tito's life, despite the fact that Yugoslavia's whole economic situation had become parlous since the mid-1970s, the country's decision-makers withheld knowledge of the imminent catastrophe from the President, right up until his death in 1980. In this case, well intentioned as it was, protecting *the chicken that must not know* laid the seeds (if not grains) of turmoil that resulted later in the horrors of ethnic cleansing. In today's West, the chicken that does/ must not know can be seen in society's attitude to children. Paedophilia is a recurrent news scare because, confronted with widespread media depictions of violence and sexuality, adults compensate by emotionally over-investing in children as guarantors of innocence that need protecting at all costs. This was evident in the demonization of the two British ten-year-old boys Jon Venables and Robert Thompson, who in

1993 abducted, tortured, and killed the almost three-year-old James Bulger. The tabloid media's febrile reporting of the crime was infused by a sense of how the youth of the killers had undermined and disturbed the public's notion of childhood innocence.

A brief consideration of *Forrest Gump* (Robert Zemeckis 1994), an ideologically less-than-innocent film about innocence, brings together the ticklishly symbolic role of the feather and the chicken that doesn't know. The movie opens with a long, technically sophisticated, shot of a feather floating in the sky. It falls towards the ground, billows across a street, and comes to rest at the feet of Forrest Gump sitting at a bus stop. Gump picks up the feather and places it in a book, which he then locks away in his suitcase. The feather is further 'book-ended' when, in the film's final scene, the feather's journey is reversed. It falls out of the book that Gump has now passed on to his son, and floats away from his feet into the sky until it covers the camera lens ending the film. Superficially, the feather represents the contingency of life that the film purports to represent. However, on closer inspection, the literal initial locking away of the feather occurs metaphorically throughout the movie in a troubling fashion. The clumsy use of the feather as a crude Hollywoodized signification of Milan Kundera's 'unbearable lightness of being' is soon weighed down by the movie's rather more heavy-handed value system sonorously evinced in the repeated cliché, 'life's a box of chocolates' (a Lacanian *point de capiton* [quilting point]). For Žižek, Gump is 'the impossible *pure subject of ideology* . . . the ideal of a subject in whom Ideology would function flawlessly' (*Indivisible Remainder*: 200). He represents 'this perfect "vanishing mediator," the very opposite of the Master (the one who symbolically registers an event by nominating it, by inscribing it into the big Other): Gump is presented as the innocent bystander who, by just doing what he does, unknowingly sets in motion a shift of historical proportions' (Žižek 2005b website). Unlike Gump, who is blissfully ignorant about the import of the history-making events he inadvertently participates within, those who do attempt to cognitively map life's vicissitudes meet a harsh fate – most emblematically, Jenny, who dies of AIDS. Speaking at her graveside at the end of the film, Gump says, 'I don't know if we each have a destiny, or if we're all just floating around accidental – like on a breeze – but I, I think maybe it's both.' Gump's graveside articulation of Hollywood ideology excludes Marx's radical third option: that we make our own fate, but not in conditions of our own choosing.

The character Forrest Gump is a pure subject of ideology in the obvious sense that he acts as an unquestioning cipher for a conservative zeitgeist – an American Dream in which there is no room for free-love hippies and Vietnam War protesters. The film *Forrest Gump* is a pure subject of ideology in the more abstract thematic sense. It is a heart-warming tale of an idiot-savant that subjects its audience to the ideology of the American Dream in an apparently non-ideological fashion. Such mediated ideological subjects/subjections are reinforced throughout capitalist society by their inanimate corollaries. A sublime *object* of ideology can be found in the form of the Kentucky Fried Chicken (Faustian) bargain bucket lid available in the UK in November 2009 and upon which was printed the following:

Give And Help Save Lives

World Hunger Relief 2009

To donate go to:
www.fromhungertohope.com

The function of this object is to desublimate ideology into a seemingly natural everyday item. It reverses the import of Marx's dictum so that today we prefer not to make our own fate in conditions of our own choosing. The relief of world hunger is to be achieved through the consumption of over-sized portions of deep-fried food. Wilfully oblivious to the structural causes of world famine, the philanthropically minded Western consumer who does not want to know is safeguarded by Forrest Gump-like ignorance. We charitably purchase factory-farmed birds so that political chickens do not come home to roost.

HARI'S GAME: REFUSING TO BE TICKLED

To the academic world's small population of postmodernists, Slavoj Žižek – a shambling, rambling Slovenian philosopher – is a folk hero. At any lecture podium, any time, anywhere, he will emit hazy clouds of gaseous theory with the speedy intensity and comic riffs of Bill Hicks. . . . Žižek is the biggest box-office draw postmodernists have ever had, their best punch at the bestseller lists. (Hari 2007)

In the above excerpt from a review article of Astra Taylor's biographical documentary film *Žižek!*, pejoratively entitled 'Pseud's Corner',[5] the British journalist Johann Hari typifies the manner in which Žižek is used by some in the media as a figure upon which to project their anxiety for unfamiliar ideas and their distrust of unashamedly enthusiastic theorizing. Žižek is sneered at for being somehow simultaneously shambling and rambling yet also a speedy, intense, and skilled comic. Similarly, in the first sentence postmodernism is scorned for the insignificance of its 'small population', but then, later, at least some of the antipathy towards Žižek appears to be motivated by a dislike at the way in which his output has approached mainstream levels of accessibility. Most discombobulating of all for Hari is Žižek's alleged lack of belief:

> What does Slavoj Žižek believe? What does he argue for? Such obvious questions are considered vulgar among postmodernists. When you first look through the more than 50 books he has written, it is almost impossible to find an answer. It seems he seeks to splice Karl Marx with the notoriously incomprehensible French psychoanalyst Jacques Lacan, slathering on top an infinite number of pop-cultural references. . . . When you peel back the patina of postmodernism, there is old-fashioned philo-tyrannical nonsense here. . . . these very positions are admissions that postmodernism is merely an unserious confection by intellectuals. It leads nowhere except to demoralisation and disaffection. (ibid.)

Passing over the hint of hysteria reflected in the repetition, throughout the piece, of the postmodernism canard, Hari's mode of objection inadvertently but clearly illustrates the sort of ideological operation frequently addressed in Žižek's work. An individual threat to the media's normally veiled ideological underpinnings (Žižek) is transformed into an 'eternal' figure (the postmodern thinker). Steven Poole, a journalist peer of Hari's, identifies both the fundamental inaccuracy and displacement activity involved in the postmodernist slur when he rhetorically asks:

> Does it matter that Žižek himself has repeatedly explicitly denounced what he understands to be 'postmodernism'? Does it even matter that what is often taken to be the manifesto of these continental clowns, Jean-François Lyotard's

The Postmodern Condition (1979), is at least as much a
lament for as a celebration of what it describes? Indeed,
is not the term 'postmodern' and its cognates these days
rather like the phrase 'politically correct', existing purely as
a handy boo-term for idiots? (Poole 2007)

Since two of the main theoretical influences upon Žižek
– Kant and Hegel – are, at the most basic factual chrono-
logical level, difficult to describe as postmodern, and almost
as difficult to portray in theoretical terms as relativist (Kant
giving us the *categorical imperative* as the touchstone of the
ethically unambiguous and Hegel producing the distinctly
non-relativist notion of the *Absolute Idea*), deeply mistaken
as it is, the most likely source of the charge of postmodern
relativism lies in Žižek's adoption and adaptation of psychoanalytical thought and its openness to the structuring power
of nothingness – the intangible gaps and absences in our
individual lives and social interactions that nevertheless have
profoundly important practical effects.

ŽIŽEK'S TICKLISH TRUTH

In a country where you can say anything, even the truth,
the outcome is that, no matter what they say, it has no kind
of effect whatsoever. (Lacan 2008: 49)

Pontius Pilate had no luck, and nor do I. He said a thing
that is really commonplace and easy to say: 'What is truth?'
He had no luck, he asked the question of Truth itself. That
got him into all kinds of bother, and he does not have a
good reputation. (ibid.: 16)

As Lacan suggests, truth is an innately ticklish proposition.
The protean nature of Žižek's theoretical short-circuits

serves a consistent basic purpose: to uncover the manner in which truth is routinely obfuscated and elided within the media. Žižek's analytical sophistication lies in his recognition of the interrelated nature of truth and concealment and how this combined nature is processed through the media's naturalized form of concealment through revelation, its 'medium is the message' conflation of form and content – the ideological wheelbarrow. Freud's fundamental rule of the analytical procedure was adherence to absolute candour buttressed by an 'analytic attitude' based upon an openness to considering curious (but no less true) links between otherwise apparently unrelated phenomena. This combination of candour and openness is what is needed to realize that '[c]oncealment doesn't merely obscure truth. It contains it. Truth, untruth, revelation, and concealment each implicate the others' (Thompson 1994: 67). Žižek is directly influenced by a Heideggerian approach 'based on the oldest name for truth in Greek philosophy: *aletheia*. The key to this word lies in *lethe*, which conveys a number of closely related ideas: concealment, hiddenness, veiledness, coveredness. The *a-* has the function of reversing the connotation of hiding something' (ibid.: 62). Signally lacking the openness of the psychoanalytical method, the methodologically 'correct' strictures of 'social science' have little or no relevance to *aletheia* and the sometimes uncomfortable reality that fantasy is replete with significant meaning.

To describe the ideological consequences of this preference for correctness over truth, Žižek is fond of quoting Lacan's paradoxical formulation '*les non-dupes errent*' (the non-duped err), which he explicates as 'those who do not let themselves be caught in the symbolic deception/fiction and continue to believe their eyes are the ones who err most' (Žižek 2005c website). In a related vein, Heidegger opines that '[m]an's flight from the mystery toward what is readily available, onward from one current thing to the next, passing the mystery by – this is *erring*' (cited in Thompson 1994: 67). Here Heidegger and Žižek both highlight the limitations of conventional evidence-based empirical research that struggles to deal with the fact that not only can the actual be false but the false can be actual. Žižek's notion of erring alludes to the power of symbolic fictions that add a further layer of experiential variegation to our usual conception of the relationship between appearances and their possibly deceptive nature. Thus, as the case of the metal known as fool's gold demonstrates, something may be actual (it physically exists) but false (it is not the precise metal that people actually desire). Symbolic fictions also introduce the reverse situation: something may not actually exist in any physical sense but it nevertheless truly has effects. This can be witnessed in the case of a judge who, although perhaps physically weak and unadmirable as a person, becomes a powerful figure of respect as soon as he or she dons the robes of office and enters a courtroom, or, as King Lear puts it: 'Thou hast seen a farmer's dog bark at a beggar? . . . And the creature run from the cur? There thou mightst behold the great image of authority: a dog's obeyed in office' (*King Lear*, Act IV, Sc. vi).

Žižek's media analysis avoids the error of insensitivity to the power of symbolic efficiency. Rather than fleeing from the mystery towards the readily available, he takes the readily available and finds the mystery within it. In this sense, he answers Siegfried Kracauer's complaint that too often cultural commentators 'avoid the most urgent human concerns, dragging the exotic into daily life rather than searching for the exotic within the quotidian . . .' (Kracauer 1995: 311). The Kantian and Hegelian philosophy Žižek draws upon uses error to interrogate the inherently illusionary nature of reality:

The critical 'system' amounts to a presentation (*Darstellung*) of the systematic a priori structure of all possible/thinkable 'errors' in their immanent necessity ... what we get at the end is not the Truth that overcomes/sublates the preceding illusions – the only truth is the inconsistent edifice of the logical interconnection of all possible illusions. ... This shift from the representation of metaphysical Truth to the truth of the shift from error to error ... this 'dialogic' process of truth emerging as the critical denouncing of the preceding illusion .... (Gabriel and Žižek 2009: 2)

In the context of the relationship between appearance and truth, a common misunderstanding of Baudrillard's notion of simulation is that it refers to the false, the non-real. The precise meaning of the concept refers to a state of being in which the relationship between the real and the representation has broken down to produce an inextricable mixture in which it no longer makes any sense to distinguish between what is real and what is fake. Baudrillard's related notion of the *hyperreal* is anything but illusionary; rather, he defines it as that which is more real than the real itself – the sort of *über*-reality typified by an Irish theme bar that exhibits more Irishness than one could find in Ireland itself (perhaps an understatement if one considers today's Irish self-theming of Dublin as a tourist destination). Faced with the paradox of the reality of illusion, in an appropriately counter-intuitive fashion, Žižek probes as practically as possible the ways in which reality is experienced via the inconsistent edifice of illusions. His rooting of concepts in an openness to reality's truly ambiguous nature means that '[w]hen we try to measure them against the real thing, they befuddle as much as enlighten. Perhaps what is real isn't so categorical. Like existence itself, we determine its efficacy by degrees. It's more or less what it seems' (Thompson 1994: 49), or, as we shall now see, sometimes nothing can be very significant.

MUCH ADO ABOUT NOTHING

Lear. . . . what can you say to draw
A third more opulent than your sisters?
Speak.
Cord. Nothing, my lord.
Lear. Nothing!
Cord. Nothing.
Lear. Nothing will come of nothing.
Speak again.
(*King Lear*, Act I, Sc. i)

At the beginning of Shakespeare's play, King Lear is fatefully dismissive of the power of nothing. Cordelia's sisters are effusive in their expressions of love for their father, but that effusiveness is at least partially informed by calculations of what would be politic to say in order to ensure their share of the family inheritance. By contrast, Cordelia's silence is much more complex than mere utilitarian calculation; her failure to speak incorporates her values as to what constitutes proper filial duty, the potential honour of her future husband, and a firmly held set of principles as to what is correct and proper to say in public about one's genuine love for another and what is best left unsaid. *Contra* Lear's claim that 'nothing will come of nothing', Shakespeare proceeds to build one of his most significant plays on this misleadingly superficial act of saying nothing. Elsewhere in Shakespeare, the antic disposition Hamlet adopts towards first Ophelia and then Guildenstern is also built upon a sensitivity to the power of nothing:

Ham. Lady, shall I lie in your lap?
Oph. No, my Lord.
Ham. I mean, my head upon your lap?
Oph. Ay, my Lord.
Ham. Do you think I meant country matters?
Oph. I think nothing, my Lord.
Ham. That's a fair thought to lie between maids' legs.
Oph. What is, my Lord?
Ham. Nothing.

(Act III, Sc. ii)

Ham. The body is with the king, but the king is not with
the body. The king is a thing –
Guild. A *thing*, my lord?
Ham. Of nothing.

(Act IV, Sc. ii)

Contra King Lear and in keeping with Freud's emphasis upon
the ability of jokes to reveal the elemental psychopathologies
of everyday life, the antic disposition of Žižek's media analysis is highly sensitive to the positive, generative properties of
what may appear to be only gaps and absences. In Sartre's
L'être et le néant (*Being and Nothingness*), no-thing-ness is
what constructs us as human beings: 'Consciousness is a
being, the nature of which is to be conscious of the nothingness of its being' (Sartre 1966 [1943]: 86). Nothingness is far
from being pure affectless neutrality; it is a fundamental part
of the way in which symbolic culture (of which the media
is obviously a particularly strong part) constitutes our social
reality: 'It is evident that non-being always appears within
the limits of a human expectation. . . . It would be in vain to
deny that negation appears on the original basis of a relation
to man in the world' (ibid.: 38). A crucial role is played in
Žižek's work by the additional gap that exists between the

significance of the philosophical substance of the questions he raises and the often humorous nature of the raw material he garners from the media.

We have previously seen how the joke embodies subtle psychological elements in a deceptively insignificant form.[6] Spontaneous but intricate processes take place for the both the joker and the audience stemming from 'this attaching of sense ... this discovering of truth', and leading from 'this granting of consequences' to 'the consciousness or impression of relative nothingness' (Freud 2001d [1905]: 12). What is *not* said within a joke is often the most important part: 'A joke says what it has to say, not always in few words, but in *too* few words – that is, in words that are insufficient by strict logic or by common modes of thought and speech. It may even actually say what it has to say by not saying it' (ibid.: 9). Moving from *King Lear* to the US hit comedy sitcom *Seinfeld* serves to demonstrate, by imitation, not only the productive nature of Žižek's high/low culture short-circuit method but also the paradoxical power and comedic ticklishness of nothing. *Seinfeld* is based upon the quotidian lives of a group of friends from Manhattan. A typically labyrinthine episode entitled 'The Pitch' provides an interestingly reflexive take on TV's inner workings and its relationship to nothing. The characters Jerry and George decide to pitch their idea of a sitcom about the daily lives of a group of friends to an NBC executive. When Jerry asks George what the show is about, George replies, 'It's about nothing ... Absolutely nothing ... Everybody's doing something, we'll do nothing.' In other words, the content of this particular sitcom episode is the form of the sitcom itself. The gaps between fiction, reality, and fictionalized representations of non-fictional reality are used to generate humour from 'a show about nothing'.

Much of the comedy mileage in *Seinfeld* is derived from the sustained exploration of this essentially empty initial premise.

In the subsequent *Curb Your Enthusiasm* made by *Seinfeld*'s real-life producer Larry David (LD1) and based upon the fictionalized day-to-day life of Larry David the producer of *Seinfeld* (LD2 played by LD1), the comic effect is further fuelled by additional densely tangled iterations that deliberately blur the boundaries between fictional and non-fictional formats. This is particularly evident in LD1/LD2's reintroduction of the original *Seinfeld* set and cast within *Curb*'s Season 7 (Pilkington 2009). Here, the real physical setting for a fictional representation (the production set of *Seinfeld*) of a purportedly non-fictional, prosaic premise (the everyday lives of four friends) has now merged with the subsequent fictional spin-off TV series (*Curb*) based upon a portrayal (the Larry David of *Curb* – LD2) of the real-life producer (LD1) of the fictional *Seinfeld*. At one particularly hyperreal point in *Curb*, the actor Jason Alexander, who played the George Costanza character in *Seinfeld*, is acting as the purportedly non-fictional Jason Alexander in (the nevertheless still fictional) *Curb*. Alexander makes ironic comments to LD2 about his character Costanza. He tells LD2 that he doesn't want to play Costanza again, describing him as a 'jerky, schmucky little character' – the joke being that Costanza was originally based upon the same LD1 that is now playing LD2. Yet further dense inter-textuality results when, in another episode, LD1 plays LD2 from *Curb* standing in for the *Seinfeld* Costanza who was originally based upon LD1. Whilst theorists of simulation such as Baudrillard are routinely accused of being too abstract and esoteric, media content provides these very 'clear' manifestations of highly convoluted modes of simulation. The entire Season 7 of *Curb* is organized around the *Seinfeld* reunion, which is planned, produced, and even shown in short fragments, but never delivered in its entirety, thus providing another example of the central, organizing role of absence in 'a show about nothing'.[7]

THE UNBEARABLE LIGHTNESS OF BEING
CAPITALIST

... every particular position is haunted by its implicit
universality, which undermines it. Capitalism is not just
universal in itself, it is universal for itself, as the tremendous
actual corrosive power which undermines all particular
lifeworlds, cultures and traditions, cutting across them,
catching them in its vortex. It is meaningless to ask 'Is this
universality true or a mask of particular interests?' This
universality is directly actual as universality, as the negative
force of mediating and destroying all particular content.
(*Violence*: 132)

Žižek's philosophical interpretation of the negative, path-
ologically universalizing nature of capitalism produces
profoundly practical political and economic insights. The
anomalously concrete abstractions that result from the capitalist vortex are experienced by workers around the world
in the form of very real effects (unemployment, low wages,
etc.), even if the root causes become difficult, if not impossible, to attribute directly. Žižek points out that this global
dimension of capitalism 'can only be formulated at the level
of truth-without-meaning, as the "Real" of the global market
mechanism' (ibid.: 68). In philosophical terms, this situation
can be described as a Hegelian ' "objective excess" – the direct
reign of abstract universality' (ibid.: 12). The very quality of
philosophy that makes it most vulnerable to charges of esoteric irrelevance to today's pressing needs also makes it the
most insightful tool with which to understand the *de facto*
colonization of contemporary mediated life by an abstract
universality that has become so socially pervasive because of
its very intangibility. Philosophy recaptures meaning from
this ethereal yet hugely destructive vortex in which causality

is reduced to flickering intimations – the evanescent numbers on the plasma screens of the money markets.

It is ironic that for a social system based upon a hard-nosed appreciation of non-utopian practicalities, capitalism is experienced as this remorselessly universalizing process of abstraction. Innately insensitive to local context, capitalism *detotalizes* any particular meaning; it is devoted to eliminating materially based idiosyncracies:

> Capitalism . . . for all its crass materialism, is secretly allergic to matter. No individual object can fulfil its voracious appetite as it hunts its way restlessly from one to the other, dissolving each of them to nothing in doomed pursuit of its ultimate desire. . . . It is a culture shot through with fantasy, idealist to its core. (Eagleton 2003: 165)

The under-acknowledged ideological role of the media is the manner in which it serves as a system (for Baudrillard, a totalitarian semiotic order) that presents this abstract universality to us as society's natural backdrop. Thus, although nominally neutral data-transmitters, computers act as vehicles for the reality-suffocating economic fantasy at capitalism's heart, so that: 'Bill Gates has commonly celebrated cyberspace as opening up the prospect of what he calls "friction-free capitalism" – this expression renders perfectly the social fantasy which underlies the ideology of cyberspace capitalism, of a wholly transparent, ethereal medium of exchange in which the last trace of material inertia vanishes' (*Plague*: 156). Instead of passively accepting the 'friction-free' rhetoric, the true job of the cultural analyst is to traverse this economic fantasy in order to be able to discern the irreducible inter-relationship of matter and its abstractions. Žižek's recourse to Kant, Hegel, and Lacan enables a precise appreciation of how the commodity form suppresses the particularity of our immediate surroundings, conflating, as it does, the immaterial and the material to produce the im/materiality of cybernetic capitalism (see Taylor and Harris 2005).

Instead of treating media fictions as an easily separable realm distinct from prosaic reality, the radical psychoanalytical insight is that 'truth is structured like fiction'. Reality is *only* accessible through our subjectivized fictional and fantastical engagements with it. Whilst, for some, this type of reasoning represents the epitome of academic otherworldliness, real-world financiers have no qualms taking the power of fantasy seriously so that they may profit so liberally from friction-free capitalism. Writing just before the most recent full-blown international economic crisis occurred, Žižek evoked 'the mad, self-enhancing circulation of capital, whose solipsistic path of parthenogenesis reaches its apogee in today's meta-reflexive speculations on futures' (*Violence*: 10). Conventional media commentary upon the world economic system can be relatively critical in the sense that it may use images like an out-of-control juggernaut to decry market fluctuations. However, it soon betrays its ideologically unsophisticated understanding of fantasy's political power by immediately trying to flesh out the abstract facts and figures that accompany discussion of recession with interviews and images of adversely affected 'real' people. Informed by a philosophy of dialectical materialism that recognizes the dynamic relationship between matter and abstraction, Žižek seeks to reclaim the power of speculation from the speculators rather than censure them for failing to adequately take into account the real effects of their actions on ordinary people's lives. He highlights the dialectic that media analysis routinely fails to register: 'The problem is that this "abstraction" is not only in our financial speculators' misperception of social reality, but that it is "real" in the precise sense of determining the structure of the material social processes

...' (ibid.: 10–11). Simply put, one cannot properly understand material reality without realizing the role played by immaterial factors.

There is a certain historical fatefulness in the fact that whilst Marxist theory has become almost a shorthand phrase for utopian wishful thinking and/or academic irrelevance, its actual descriptive ability has never been stronger. In fact, it could be argued that Marx's original analysis of the capitalist process was, if anything, too understated: 'Do phenomena usually designated as those of virtual capitalism (the futures trade and similar abstract financial speculations) not point towards the reign of the "real abstraction" at its purest, far more radical than in Marx's time?' (ibid.: 12). The apparent contradiction contained within the notion of the 'Real of spectrality' (ibid.: 12) is indeed only apparent. A full understanding of what it is to experience reality as a human requires acknowledgement that the spectral has very real effects. The theoretical basis of this crucial point is Lacan's distinction between reality – our quotidian understanding of everyday physical reality and the people who interact within it – and the *Real*, his psychoanalytical notion of that which resists ready symbolization, the stubborn kernel of existence that we cannot fully conceptualize or fully verbalize. In the specific context of the global financial meltdown, 'reality' is the social reality of people involved in personal interactions and in the productive processes that create commodities, whereas the Real is 'the inexorable "abstract", spectral logic of capital that determines what goes on in [that] social reality' (ibid.: 11). Thus, whilst workers may rub shoulders with each other on the factory floor, their ultimate fate is dependent upon the spectral logic of those rapidly changing digital figures on screens thousands of miles away.

Although Baudrillard's and Žižek's critical analyses of simulation meet with dismissals like Hari's previously

encountered jibe of an 'unserious confection', it is arguably their detractors who exhibit cynical relativism through
actions that betray their lack of belief in the very reality
principle they claim to uphold against the depredations of
postmodern theory. The corporate form of this cynical disavowal can be seen in Starbucks' recent efforts to present
elements of its franchise as independent neighbourhood
coffee shops:

> In a diversion from its usual mixture of stripped wood decor
> and bland artwork, Starbucks is opening a store in its home
> city of Seattle intended to capture the vibe of a beatnik
> coffee hangout – and disguise the fact that drinkers are in a
> Starbucks. The store will be called 15th Avenue Coffee and
> Tea in an apparent attempt to mimic a local, independent
> coffee shop.
>
> A Starbucks spokeswoman says the place will have a
> 'mercantile' look with open bins of coffee beans and manual
> grinding machines. There will be live music and poetry
> performances. At least two other re-hashed outlets are on
> the way in Seattle as chairman Howard Schultz tries push-
> ing Starbucks back towards its artsy roots.
>
> Steve Gotham, an analyst at marketing consultancy
> Allegra Strategies, thinks this is a smart move as custom-
> ers look for differentiation among branded coffee houses:
> 'The issue of localness and local relevance has some way to
> go – it's a consumer trend more operators need to tap into.'
> (Clark 2009)

Both the marketing consultants and the customers availing
themselves of the neo-mercantile atmosphere of carefully
culturally re-engineered shops know that genuine 'local-
ness' and 'local relevance' cannot be corporately generated,
but proceed as if it can. Nevertheless, for consumers, the

illusionary experience becomes more desirable and 'natural' than any notion of an original – the serious philosophical issue at the heart of Larry David's playfulness and George Costanza's pitch.

CONCLUSION: SPIRIT IS A BONE(R)

... the *being of Spirit is a bone*. (Hegel 1977 [1807]: 208)

What is the lightest object in the world? The penis, because it is the only one that can be raised by a mere thought. (*Ticklish Subject*: 382–3)

In the above quotations, Hegel gnomically encapsulates the inextricable link between the abstract and the material that Shakespeare so dramatically evoked in Hamlet's contemplation of poor Yorick's skull, whilst Žižek tumescently 'fleshes' out the ticklish high/low nature our existential condition and the paradoxically physical effects of the immaterial. A large part of the media's implicit ideology is based upon the control and manipulation of the generative and foundational power of nothingness, gaps and absences. Explicit reflexive engagement with the nothingness at the heart of the symbolic order, however, tends to be safely circumscribed within such fictional (albeit hugely inventive) forms as *Curb Your Enthusiasm* – a revealing title that, as a superegoic prohibition, acts as a negative corollary to Žižek's more empowering injunction to 'enjoy your symptom!' (*Symptom*). Žižek's philosophical significance stems from his affinity with George Costanza and Larry David's phenomenological spin on the standard sitcom: they all recognize that much substance, whether comedic or tragic, does indeed come from nothing. Far from being a postmodern relativist, Žižek seeks truth, though '[n]ot by running after "objective" truth, but by holding onto the truth about the position from which one speaks' (*Lost Causes*: 3). To put it another way, whilst the chicken may not know the difference between a madman and a grain of corn, and Forrest Gump thinks life is like a box of chocolates, Žižek understands when the otherwise diaphanous nature of a kinky feather, fleetingly tumescent thought, flickering digital figures on a capitalist's plasma screen, and tickling s(h)tick weighs heavy with significance.

3

BIG (BR)OTHER
Psychoanalysing the Media

INTRODUCTION: MEDIATING REALITY

... the 'normal' human sexual act has the structure of a
double masturbation: each partner is masturbating with a
real partner. However, the gap between the raw reality of
copulation and its fantasmatic supplement can no longer be
closed; all variations and displacements of sexual practices
that follow are so many desperate attempts to restore the
balance of the two. (*Parallax*: 12)

Intercourse ... is sometimes a satisfactory substitute for
masturbation. But it takes a lot of imagination for it to
work. (Karl Kraus in Szaz 1990: 154)

Even such a stalwart critic of psychoanalysis as Karl Kraus
recognized the structuring role played in prosaic reality
by fantasy. Žižek's above matching comment shows how
even the sexual act, perhaps our rawest, most animalistic,

encounter with unadulterated reality, is actually suffused with fantasy. The concept of fantasy is normally understood as an imaginary element to be distinguished from reality 'proper'; Žižek's point is that this is an excessively simplistic distinction. Without its 'fantasmatic supplement', undeniably real aspects of human experience like sexuality could not exist since we would be unable to move beyond the most basic act of animalistic copulation. Sex is a particularly direct (literally embodied) encounter with reality, but fantasy plays the same structuring role in all our social encounters. Žižek's frequent recourse to German Idealist philosophers, particularly Kant and Hegel, combined with his additional recourse to psychoanalysis enables him to provide a highly variegated conceptual account of what our common-sense notion of 'reality' excludes. It gives him the capacity to explore the abstract topography of the various gaps and absences that structure reality and how they are processed within various mediated forms such as TV, cinema, and cyberspace.

THE REAL

The Real is what lies beyond the immediate reach of language. It is capitalized to distinguish it from the conventional notion of *r*eality, which is used as a catch-all phrase for 'everything we consciously experience'. The Real cannot be grasped, it cannot be measured. It is experienced only through its effects and affects. A minimum of mental health requires us to mediate reality's brute facticity and sensuousness via a series of necessary idealizations. Human language is premised upon our need to filter out the excess sensory data so that, in the semantic example previously used, 'treeness' can displace the myriad, much more accurate, but impractically inexhaustible, detailed descriptions of each individual tree we might wish to describe. Psychotic mental states are frequently associated with a failure to filter adequately this specificity of our sensory perceptions. Roquentin, the protagonist of Sartre's *La Nausée* (*Nausea*) (1983 [1938]), provides a literary case in point. In a germinal expression of existentialist thought, Roquentin is hyper-sensitively oppressed by the pure physicality of a chestnut tree; its root at his feet overwhelms him with its gross specificity. In a novelistic representation of Kant's *ding-an-sich* (the thing in itself) and Lacan's *Das Ding* (The Thing), to Roquentin's eyes, the root oozes with life – the ultimately inexpressible/unrepresentable vital force of nature, its rooty 'thingness':

> That root, with its colour, its shape, its frozen movement, was . . . beneath all explanation. Each of its qualities escaped from it a little, flowed out of it, half-solidified, almost became a thing; each one was *superfluous in* the root, and the whole stump now gave me the impression of rolling a little outside itself, denying itself, losing itself in a strange excess. I scraped my heel against that black claw: I should have liked to peel off a little of the bark. For no particular reason, out of defiance, to make the absurd pink of an abrasion appear on the tanned leather: to *play* with the absurdity of the world. But when I took my foot away, I saw that the bark was still black . . . . It *resembled* a colour but also . . . a bruise or again a secretion, a yoke – and something else, a smell for example, it melted into a smell of wet earth, of warm, moist wood, into a black smell spread like varnish over that sinewy wood, into a taste of sweet, pulped fibre. I didn't *see* that black in a simple way: sight is an abstract invention, a cleaned-up simplified idea, a human idea. That black, a weak, amorphous presence, far surpassed sight, smell, and taste. But that richness became confusion and finally ceased to be anything at all because it was too much. (Sartre 1983 [1938]: 186–7)

Žižek explains the difference between the Real and reality in terms of the experience of witnessing extreme violence or explicit sexual content. The original experience becomes 'derealized', almost hallucinatory in retrospect, so that when one attempts to return to 'normal' reality it is difficult to think of the two realms as being the same: 'This is what Lacan is aiming at in his distinction between reality and the Real: we cannot ever acquire a complete, all-encompassing sense of reality – some part of it must be affected by the "loss of reality", deprived of the character of "true reality", and this fictionalized element is precisely the traumatic Real' (*Real Tears*: 66).

A vivid illustration of this profoundly necessary and inescapably phantastical aspect of the Real is contained within the film *Good* (Vicente Amorim 2008). Vigo Mortensen plays the character of John Halder, a German academic at the time of the Nazi Party's rise to power. Music plays a constant, tangential presence in his life: for example, his wife (whom he leaves for a younger mistress in one of a series of moral lapses) mitigates her mental illness by constantly playing the piano, thereby providing a soundtrack to the daily domestic chores Halder is left to deal with. Throughout the film, he keeps fooling himself that things aren't so bad, to the extent that he almost inadvertently finds himself occupying a senior role in the Nazi Party whilst still in denial as to its ultimate nature. It is only very belatedly when he goes to one of the death camps in search of a Jewish friend he had earlier failed to help that the scales finally fall from his eyes. Appropriately, this occurs the precise moment at which he hears the musical scales from a bedraggled musical quartet of prisoners. It is only in this final scene of the film that he comes to terms with the true significance of the situation and, crying, he whispers to himself 'It's real' as, in the closing shot, the isolated sound of music is slowly enveloped by the screams of incoming prisoners and the vicious barking of guard-dogs.

The Lacanian Real that consistently informs Žižek's work contrasts fundamentally with conventional, common-sense notions of reality. What seems to be Halder's day-to-day life as a Nazi Party *apparatchik* is actually a fantasy in which he denies the surrounding evil to himself. Only when he hears the non-prosaic, fantastical music is he shocked out of his defensively delusional over-identification with his immediate reality and able truly to feel the full enormity of the Nazi horror from which he has hitherto shielded himself, suffering as he was from the fright of shedding real tears.[1]

Like the German Idealist philosophy of Hegel, Kant, Schelling, etc., with its focus upon the power of the non-material – the abstract, the ideal, the negative – Lacan describes a profoundly important structural relationship between an individual and his or her environment which is, in-and-of-itself, without physical substance. The human condition is caught between the Scylla of an overwhelming ontological facticity of brute materiality (Roquentin's confrontation with the chestnut tree) and the Charybdis of an ineffably immaterial Real (Halder's Damascene revelation). Hence arises the need for a symbolic order with which to navigate between the two extremes. However, this comes at the price of needing to recognize 'the impossibility inscribed into the heart of language: its failure to grasp the Real' (*They Know*: xiv). This is why Halder requires the intervention of music for his revelation.

THE SYMBOLIC

As previously described, our entry into the symbolic order comes at the cost of castration, our unavoidable inability to describe fully what we have left behind so that we are able to enter into the symbolic realm. In the following extract from

What is Literature? Sartre highlights the inverse relationship between our ability to conceptualize and sensuously experience – one tends to be gained at the expense of the other.

> As Merleau-Ponty has pointed out in *The Phenomenology of Perception*, there is no quality of sensation so bare that it is not penetrated with significance. But the dim little meaning which dwells within it, a light joy, a timid sadness, remains immanent or trembles about it like a heat mist; it *is* colour or sound. . . . It is true that one might, by convention, confer the value of signs upon them. Thus, we talk the language of flowers. But if, after the agreement, white roses signify 'fidelity' to me, the fact is that I have stopped seeing them as roses. My attention cuts through them to aim beyond them at this abstract virtue. I forget them. I no longer pay attention to their mossy abundance, to their sweet stagnant odour. I have not even perceived them. (Sartre 2001 [1948]: 2)

Sartre's existentialism was an on-going struggle with this vexing problem of how to define one's self-hood when confronted by the otherwise overwhelming arbitrariness and frustrating ineffability of our being-in-the-world. This ineffability can take the form of either the gossamer-thin subtlety of the above 'timid sadness' or the oozing excess encountered by Roquentin. The loss of a rose's 'sweet stagnant odour' poetically evokes the experiential price to be paid for entry into the symbolic order of efficient communication.

THE IMAGINARY

The Imaginary describes the illusion of false wholeness, the misleadingly stable and non-antagonistic. It is a phenomenological category manifested in the media coverage of the

Allied invasion of Iraq. In addition to the previously cited 'Mission Accomplished' press conference upon the US aircraft carrier USS *Lincoln* on 1 May 2003, other premature images of victory include the draping of a Stars and Stripes flag over the face of a Saddam statue. This represented a geopolitically important premonition of a failure to know what it is that we see caused by the Western media's unhealthy relationship to the spectacle. The disastrous display of overconfidence prefigured the subsequently catastrophic failure to produce the requisite level of post-war contingency planning. Immediately after the draping of the Stars and Stripes, US troops intervened with military machinery to supplant the originally unsuccessful manual attempts of local Iraqis to pull the Saddam statue down. The manner in which the troops excluded the Iraqis had obvious parallels with US disregard for Iraqi autonomy in the occupying forces' subsequently plagued attempts at nation-building. The Imaginary represents a falsely neat resolution to the unavoidable problems encountered once we inhabit a symbolic order, and post-war Iraq bears poignant testimony to this realm's very real effects. A profound difference of perspective exists between Žižek's political philosophy, with its sustained focus upon symbolic/imaginary convolutions, and Western politicians' manipulation of the Imaginary for domestic and foreign policy purposes. For Peter Mandelson, *contra* Sartre, the red flag of socialism loses the acrid, stagnant odour of violent history. It is re-branded to become the odourless sign of a red rose that conveys florally rather than philosophically the dim little meaning of a politically etiolated party – New Labour.

THE BIG OTHER

Our experience of social reality consists of a tangled amalgamation of the above three registers. The Real needs mediating but it continues to bubble under the surface of the Symbolic and Imaginary constructions we use for that medi-ation. In order to function fully as both individuals and social beings, we need the symbolic order. This is what gives rise to the *the big Other*. At the most basic level of communication, the symbolic order imposes itself in terms of the grammati-cal rules we use in language. To these rules can be added the broader, tacit assumptions of the social background within which a language operates:

> The rules that I follow are marked by a deep split: there are rules (and meanings) that I follow blindly, out of custom, but of which, upon reflection, I can become at least partially aware (such as common grammatical rules), and there are rules that I follow, meanings that haunt me, unbeknownst to me (such as unconscious prohibitions). Then there are rules and meanings I am aware of, but have to act on the outside as if I am not aware of them – dirty or obscene innuendos which one passes over in silence in order to maintain the proper appearances. This symbolic space acts like a standard against which I can measure myself. (*How to Read Lacan*: 9; 1997c website)

Žižek humorously illustrates the simultaneously socially essential and invasively personal nature of the big Other by recourse to the tale of the poor peasant who finds himself shipwrecked with the supermodel Cindy Crawford. For want of better alternatives, Cindy is reduced to having sex with the peasant, but when, out of politeness, she asks him if he is satisfied, he makes a further request – that she dress up as his best friend, complete with fake moustache. When she does this, the peasant nudges her in the ribs and says, 'Guess what? I've just had sex with Cindy Crawford!' The point here is that there is no such thing as a purely private moment. Our most intimate acts can only take place in the shadow of this standard against which we cannot escape judging ourselves – the big Other that is always lurking phantasmatically, but no less efficiently, in the background of our consciousness. Whilst, even in a 'normal' society, the need to traverse the three registers of the Real, Imaginary, and Symbolic is unavoidable, the contemporary mediascape is distinguished by the degree to which the symbolic efficiency of the big Other has been colonized by the ultra-efficient transmission of hyperreal signs.

THE *MEDIATED* INDIVIDUAL

What passes for normal is to venerate virginity in general but thirst for its destruction in particular cases. (Kraus 2001 [1923]: 12 n100)

Pace Kraus, an irreducible tension and irresolvable gap exists between the particular phenomena/objects we encounter on an everyday basis and the universal categories we use to make sense of those particularities to ourselves and others. Our symbolic order evolves from this inescapable communicational need to mediate between our individual experience of reality and the wider social system of meaning required to sustain our individual experiences of that reality. The desire to explain this complex set of interactions accounts for Žižek's combination of psychoanalytical and philosophical theory examined in the previous two chapters. Žižek uses his philosophical understanding of the gap at the heart of being, taken from the tradition of German Idealist philosophy, and uses it to supplement his psychoanalytically informed interpretation of the constitutive gap between the individual and the social symbolic order. The result is shown to be a singularly useful theoretical method for exploring the specific ways in which the advent of media technologies with ever more sophisticated representational abilities adds further complicating levels of mediation to the symbolic order's role as the basic mediation between the particular and the universal.

Kant famously distinguishes the way an object appears to us through the mediation of the senses from the thing as it is in itself (Kant 1965 [1781]: B xxvii). For finite human beings, knowledge is limited to the way things appears to us in phenomenal reality, whereas what a thing is in and of itself remains forever inaccessible 'and completely unknown' (ibid.: A 42/B 59). For Žižek, however, Kant did not go far enough, hidebound as he was by the innate limitations of the initial distinction he had made. The appeal of Hegel for Žižek resides in the way in which he was arguably more Kant-like than Kant himself. 'It is Kant', Žižek writes, 'who goes only halfway in his destruction of metaphysics, still maintaining the reference to the Thing-in-itself as the externally inaccessible entity; Hegel is merely a radical-ized Kant, who takes the step from negative access to the Absolute to the Absolute itself as negativity' (*Parallax*: 27). According to Žižek's reading, what Hegel finds unsatisfac-tory is the fact that the Kantian philosophical revolution remains incomplete and unfulfilled.

For Kant, the thing-in-itself, although forever inacces-sible to finite human beings, is still thought of as a positive, substantive thing. Hegel finds this both inadequate and inconsistent. He therefore criticizes Kant not for insisting on the necessarily limited capacity of human knowledge or the fundamental inaccessibility of the thing-in-itself, but for wrongly presupposing that the thing-in-itself is some posi-tive, substantive thing and missing the fact that this thing is itself 'nothing but the inherent limitation of the intuited phenomena' (*Tarrying*: 39). Moreover:

Where Kant thinks that he is still dealing only with a negative presentation of the Thing, we are already in the midst
of the Thing-in-itself – for this Thing-in-itself is nothing
but this radical negativity. In other words – in a some-
what overused Hegelian speculative twist – the negative
experience of the Thing must change into the experience
of the Thing-in-itself as radical negativity. (*Sublime Object*:
205–6)[2]

In Žižek's reading of Kant through Hegel, immanent reality
is indelibly marked with a minimal difference. Paradoxically,
in order to be experienced at all, our sense of both reality and our subjective selves needs to contain an irreducible
gap, a lack from which meaningful experience can be generated. In terms of the relationship between subjects and the
external physical world that confronts and contains them,
this lack/gap can be explained in terms of the symbolic order
that we construct so that an otherwise excessively raw reality can be encountered in a meaningful, non-overwhelming
fashion.

Although the symbolic order occupies and contributes to
reality, having a concrete impact on people's lives, it cannot
be grasped physically. The *big Other* is the Lacanian term
used to describe this intangible structure, the social repository of collected and projected beliefs, which we all relate to
and rely upon. Paraphrasing Margaret Thatcher, *there is no
such thing as the individual.* What appears to be a self-contained, autonomous entity, a person-in-herself, is innately
dependent upon external elements for her own self-defini-
tion. Individuals can only exist as individuals to the extent
that they have successfully internalized an external symbolic
order – one's status as an autonomous *subject* presupposes a
state of *subjec*tion. In a media-saturated age this immaterial
mediation between the social and the individual is further

mediated by media technologies and formats, one of the most notable developments in recent years being the rise of reality TV – in particular, *Big Brother*. The manifest meaning of this format is that the individual viewer watches the external surveillance of others. However, the programme's latent meaning undermines any easy separation of the individual and the social. The format presents the act of individual surveillance as a celebratory, vote-counting, communal experience. In a similar vein, Žižek describes the essentially interconnected account of the individual's relationship to society's overarching symbolic order. For example, an authentically cynical loner is not possible; he presupposes the wider society from which he seeks to distance himself:

> . . . the Social, the field of social practices and socially held beliefs, is not simply at a different level from the individual experience, but something to which *the individual him/ herself has to relate*, which *the individual himself* has to experience as an order which is minimally 'reified,' externalized. The problem is therefore not 'how to jump from the individual to the social level?'; the problem is: *how should the external-impersonal socio-symbolic order of institutionalized practices and beliefs be structured, if the subject is to retain his 'sanity,' his 'normal' functioning?* (Take the proverbial egotist, cynically dismissing the public system of moral norms: as a rule, such a subject can only function if this system is 'out there,' publicly recognized, i.e. in order to be a private cynic, he has to presuppose the existence of naive other(s) who 'really believe.') In other words, the gap between the individual and the 'impersonal' social dimension is to be inscribed back within the individual himself: *this objective order of the social Substance exists only insofar as individuals treat it as such, relate to it as such.* (*Parallax*: 6)

Although the origins of psychoanalysis lie in a therapeutic process for individuals and German Idealism was designed to address seemingly abstract ontological questions, together they constitute highly practical aids for understanding today's immaterial but highly effective/affective social mediations – our contemporary big (Br)Other.

SYMBOLIC EFFICIENCY OR EYES WIDE SHUT IN CINEMA AND CYBERSPACE?

... the notion of the 'objectively subjective', of the semblance conceived in the 'objective' sense, designates the moment when the difference between objective reality and subjective semblance is reflected within the domain of the subjective semblance itself. What we obtain in this reflection-into-semblance of the opposition between reality and semblance is precisely the paradoxical notion of objective semblance, of 'how things really seem to me'. Therein resides the dialectical synthesis between the realm of the Objective and the realm of the Subjective – not simply in the notion of subjective appearance as the mediated expression of objective reality, but in the notion of a semblance that objectivizes itself and starts to function as a 'real semblance' (the semblance sustained by the big Other, the symbolic institution) against the mere subjective semblance of actual individuals. (Žižek 1998 website)

Although off-puttingly prolix at first glance, Žižek's above explanation of objective semblance goes straight to the heart of the powerfully combined social and individually felt impact of symbolic efficiency. Any initial difficulty with following Žižek's train of thought needs to be off-set against the complexity of the felt experience he is attempting to describe. Objective semblance is symbolically efficient. Even the most hard-nosed empiricist should be able to recognize that immaterial factors play significant roles in people's day-to-day lives. Whether it is a soldier willing to lay down his life for 'Queen and Country', or a public prosecutor eschewing a financially remunerative private practice for a less measurably rewarding sense of public service, symbols *matter* (to deliberately pun on their intertwining of material and immaterial effects). The crucial phrase in understanding Žižek's very specific use of the apparent oxymoron 'objective semblance' is the *dialectical synthesis*. This notion is essential for appreciating his application of German Idealist and psychoanalytical thought to the uncovering of the contemporary media's ideological processes and to explain the extent to which the objective and subjective realms cannot be separated out. In a profound ontological and psychological sense, these realms are mutually self-constituting.

An intertwined series of disavowed beliefs and practices pervade the reproduction of social reality. As previously pointed out, when we are confronted with a representative of the legal establishment, a judge, a police officer, etc., even though that individual may be deeply flawed as a person, they are still able to maintain symbolic authority through the weight of the office they carry. This simple observation raises a series of complex questions and implications for our understanding of how social reality works in practice. For example, whether it is the commodity fetishism of the market mechanism within capitalism or the total social dominance of the Party within Communism, it is possible for widespread cynicism about the ultimate truth value of a particular social structure to co-exist with widespread compliance. Even if, at a rational level, people disassociate themselves from the market or the Party, the various rituals and processes of social processes retain an objective functionality so that the distrusted entity can maintain and reproduce itself.

This process is premised upon 'the seemingly hair-splitting but nonetheless crucial distinction between "subjectively objective" and "objectively subjective": the Kantian transcendentally constituted reality is subjectively objective (it stands for objectivity that is subjectively constituted/mediated), while fantasy is objectively subjective (it designates an innermost subjective content, a product of fantasizing, which, paradoxically, is "desubjectivized", rendered inaccessible to the subject's immediate experience)' (Žižek 1998 website). The summary effect of this situation returns us to the inextricably mixed material/phantasmatic nature of our lived experience. Brute reality cannot escape our subjective conceptualization. The mere empirical existence of various social processes and institutions autonomously generates forms of symbolic efficiency that in turn permeate our conceptualizations, which return to affect how we act in the physical world, and so on, and so on, in a series of recursive loops ripe for the media's participation.

In Freud's *The Interpretation of Dreams* (2001a [1900]), an exhausted father grieving the death of his son falls asleep next to the coffin and dreams that the child is in the room, reproaching him with the cry 'Father, can't you see that I'm burning?' (see Zizek 2006b website). Eventually, smoke caused by a candle that is burning the shroud awakens the father from the dream. Žižek argues that this story is potentially deceptive. There is a temptation to presume that the smell of burning was incorporated into the dream so that the father could continue to sleep, and he only woke up when the strength of the smell in the actual room containing the coffin exceeded his ability to maintain it within the confines of the dream. A more alarming reading, however, is that the father woke up so that he could resume consciousness in the mourning room in order to avoid the even more traumatic experience of the fantasy in which he is unable to console his helpless son.

Stanley Kubrick's *Eyes Wide Shut* (1999) demonstrates cinema's ability to portray these sorts of lurking traumas that conventional social reality normally keeps from direct consideration. A film devoted to exploring the sexual fantasies of a couple, it ends with the Nicole Kidman character, who, when asked by her lover, played by Tom Cruise, what they should do next, responds 'Fuck.' Žižek suggests:

> The nature of the *passage à l'acte* as the false exit, as the way to avoid confronting the horror of the fantasmatic netherworld, was never so abruptly stated in a film: far from providing them with a real-life bodily satisfaction that would render superfluous all empty fantasising, the passage to the act is rather presented as a stopgap, as a desperate preventive measure aimed at keeping at bay the spectral netherworld of fantasies. It is as if her message is: let's fuck as soon as possible *in order to* stifle the thriving fantasies, before they overwhelm us again. Lacan's quip about awakening into reality as an escape from the Real encountered in the dream holds more than anywhere apropos of the sexual act itself: we do not dream about fucking when we are not able to do it – rather, we fuck in order to escape and stifle the excess of the dream that would otherwise overwhelm us. (*Real Tears*: 175)

From this perspective, we engage with media like cinema and cyberpace not *to escape from*, but rather in order *to escape to* a social reality that protects (mediates) us more effectively from the truly traumatic issues and concerns that belie our 'normal' lives.

In a move that, once again, is reminiscent of Guy Debord's previously cited observation that '[i]n a world which *really is topsy-turvy*, the true is a moment of the false' (Debord 1977 [1967]: N9), Žižek suggests that our standard understanding of social reality is inverted in relation to its cardinal truth:

In our 'society of the spectacle', in which what we experience as everyday reality more and more takes the form of
the lie made real, Freud's insights show their true value.
Consider the interactive computer games some of us play
compulsively, games which enable a neurotic weakling to
adopt the screen persona of a macho aggressor, beating up
other men and violently enjoying women. It's all too easy
to assume that this weakling takes refuge in cyberspace in
order to escape from a dull, impotent reality. But perhaps
the games are more telling than that. What if, in playing them, I articulate the perverse core of my personality
which, because of ethico-social constraints, I am not able to
act out in real life? Isn't my virtual persona in a way 'more
real than reality'? Isn't it precisely because I am aware that
this is 'just a game' that in it I can do what I would never be
able to in the real world? In this precise sense, as Lacan put
it, the Truth has the structure of a fiction: what appears in
the guise of dreaming, or even daydreaming, is sometimes
the truth on whose repression social reality itself is founded.
Therein resides the ultimate lesson of *The Interpretation of
Dreams*: reality is for those who cannot sustain the dream.
(Žižek 2006b website)

Žižek thus takes cinema, cyberspace, and the ubiquitous spread
of reality TV formats more seriously than they take themselves – highly useful pseudo-activities designed to retreat into
reality so that lurking traumas don't have to be confronted.

THE BIG OTHER AS BIG BROTHER: THE PORNOGRAPHY OF GRIEF IN WOOTTON BASSETT

The dream-work . . . only undertakes to represent the raw
material of the ideas and not the logical relations in which

they stand to one another; or at all events it reserves the liberty to disregard the latter. (Freud 2001d [1905]: 163)

> The recycling of contents and persons among sets or sit-coms, the closed-circuit coextensivity of what takes place on and in front of the tube – the way one sees oneself being seen or finds oneself in situations that might as well have been programmed – could all be analogized with Freud's original (telescopic) conception of the dream as the rerun of daytime trivia thus openly and simultaneously displayed or repressed. (Rickels 1990: 45)

The above link between descriptions of the dream as a non-logical collection of raw ideas and its processing of 'the rerun of daytime trivia thus openly and simultaneously displayed or repressed' represents an apposite summary of the ideo-logical function of a society of the spectacle in which images assume priority over logical connection and, perhaps most importantly of all, open display does not preclude simulta-neous repression. Visual media *screen* in both senses of the term: they process phenomena by both portrayal and reduc-tion. Just as Freud sought to understand the logical relations between dream images, so Žižek seeks to trace the logical ideological components of the media's screening of nomi-nally unrelated, non-ideological imagery. In this context, the trauma to be confronted lies less in the overwhelming solidity of reality as recounted in Roquentin's confrontation with the chestnut tree and more in the potentially discom-bobulating lack of a corresponding hardness to the self that perceives the tree:

> Lacan's point is not that, behind the multiplicity of phantas-matic identities, there is a hard core of some 'real Self', we are dealing with a symbolic fiction, but a fiction which, for

contingent reasons that have nothing to do with its inherent structure, possesses performative power – is socially operative, structures the socio-symbolic reality in which I participate. The status of the same person, inclusive of his/her very 'real' features, can appear in an entirely different light the moment the modality of his/her relationship to the big Other changes. (*Ticklish Subject*: 330)

Subjectivity is thus based not upon any inherent structure, but rather upon the relative structural position a subject assumes within the symbolic order. Suitably entitling one of his accounts *The Plague of Fantasies*, Žižek argues that a central antagonism of our contemporary mediascape is the way in which the symbolic order's abstract performative power is exacerbated by both technologies of abstraction (e.g. digitalization) and a 'deluge of pseudo-concrete images' (*Plague*: 1). This latter phrase encapsulates the tension of the *objectively subjective*. Today we are surrounded by images with little physical, material presence, but hugely affective consequences. The subject's position within the symbolic order is mediated by the fantasies (the minimal idealizations) we are forced to create to navigate our way through that order, and the media's screening adds further layers to already deeply enmeshed processes.

Big Brother's co-opting of Orwellian concepts into a Huxleyan entertainment format indicates how full consideration of the psychoanalytical import of these processes can be foreclosed in today's mediascape. The openly overdetermined physical infrastructure of the *Big Brother* compound (the Stasi-like architecture only partially ameliorated by the festival-like organization of celebratory entries and evictions) and the similarly overdetermined entertainment format (the diary room, *Big Brother*'s disembodied vocal interjections if events threaten to become too spontaneous, etc.) distract

viewers from the less obvious ideological ramifications of the
Big Brother mentality's manifestation in wider society. An
exemplification of this critical (in both senses) understanding to be gained from Žižek's emphasis upon the negative
consequences of the media's mode of ideological screening
is provided by the small English town of Wootton Bassett.
Recently, the town has become a focal point for the UK
media's reporting of the nation's grief over the deaths of
British military personnel from on-going actions in Iraq and
Afghanistan. Initially, elderly members of the Royal British
Legion (an organization that campaigns for current and
former service personnel) and passing pedestrians semi-spon-
taneously lined the streets to pay their respects as hearses
carrying the coffins of dead soldiers passed by on their way
to a nearby military base. News reports of these displays of
respect soon led to a large, invasive media presence devoted
to capturing public grief for media consumption.

Degrees of tastelessness are obviously subjective, but
they can also follow relatively objective paths. Inhabitants
of Wootton Bassett soon found themselves playing to a
media script borrowed from emotionally incontinent *Death
of Princess Diana*-type TV productions and needing to
resist mawkish calls to rename the town's High Street the
'Highway for Heroes'. On the streets of Wootton Bassett,
the relationship to the big Other incorporated in ritualistic
grief was magnified and mediated by TV cameras to produce
a problematic ideological transference. Conditioned by saturated media coverage, the original cause of public marks of
respect, the mourning of dead soldiers returning home, was
supplanted by self-conscious displays of grief. In technical
terms, both *Big Brother* and Wootton Bassett represent the
hypostatization of the big Other. Put more simply, they represent the media's tendency to attempt to make explicit what,
by its intrinsic nature, cannot be explicitly revealed. The big

Other only exists as a non-tangible construct. The moment it is mediated to the extent that it is in *Big Brother*/Wootton Bassett, it ceases to function as the big Other. Instead, it acts as a technologized displacement mechanism with which to avoid traumatic truths.

FAILING TO MIND THE GAP: THE MEDIATED NEUROSIS OF REALITY TV

'No man is a hero to his valet': not, however, because the man is not a hero, but because the valet is a valet, whose dealings are with the man, not as a hero, but as one who eats, drinks, and wears clothes. (Hegel cited in *Fragile Absolute*: 48)

Hegel's observation that a great man's valet is too close to mundane life to appreciate his master's broader historical significance encapsulates the value of theory as a resource with which to obtain the necessary distance from a situation if the required understanding is not to be lost amidst too much empirical detail. Contemporary ideology serves to obscure the core role of representational gaps at the heart of society – it occludes the various incompletenesses and absences that, as discussed above, paradoxically create the immaterial substance of much of our lived experience. In the guise of merely presenting reality, explicit media construct it ideologically. Inhabiting an historical context in which there is a perceived loss of the big Other's symbolic efficiency, the media attempts to render social reality in ever more detailed ways via the exponential growth of a range of increasingly intrusive images. This manifests itself in the rise of reality TV, the conflation of current affairs with spectacular violence and celebrity values, and the spread of ideology that, counter-intuitively, is disguised through the very obviousness of its appearance, as previously discussed in relation to *Forrest Gump*. For Žižek, the result is that '[t]he paradoxical result of this mutation in the "inexistence of the Other" (of the growing collapse of the symbolic efficiency) is precisely the re-emergence of the different facets of a big Other which exists effectively, in the Real, and not merely as symbolic fiction' (Žižek 1997a website). The media's true perversion resides not in its increasingly explicit nature and the extent of its sexualized representations (analysed as *social porn* in Taylor 2008b and Taylor and Harris 2008), its objectification of women, etc., but rather in its unremitting fixation upon the process of constructing a symbolically efficient mediated substitute predicated upon the explicit depiction of not just sexual activity but *all* social activity.

Ontological difference is the philosophical distinction between 'what things are and the fact that they are' (*Parallax*: 23). Roquentin's nausea dramatically portrays the human experience of ontological difference as an individual's disorientating perceptual confrontation with Being's inertial implacability and his overwhelming sense of its excessively material grossness – it is beyond language's capability to convey fully the sheer unremitting facticity of the chestnut tree. Our everyday understanding of reality results from the way in which we process this traumatic Real so that we can avoid Roquentin's existential crisis. What may first appear as illusion is actually a necessary mode of human interaction with an otherwise overwhelming raw Being, so that, as Žižek puts it, we need 'the illusory status of illusion itself' (*Real Tears*: 68). The rise of reality TV signifies an over-compensation for this essential inaccessibility of the Real – heavily mediated reality is offered as an ersatz alternative. In the guise of revealing new aspects of reality, reality TV actually reinvents the encounter with the chestnut tree in a perverse new form – human concerns are presented in all their inertial stupidity and grossness.[3] Opposing reality TV's ultimately unrealistic commitment to technologized realism, Žižek's theoretical framework seeks a more sophisticated interrogation of social reality that draws from the Hegelian notion of 'concrete universality', which in its turn draws from the logic of minimal difference, 'the constitutive noncoincidence of a thing with itself' (*Parallax*: 30). To convey the practical significance of this philosophical distinction, in his book *The Fright of Real Tears*, Žižek describes how the Polish film-maker Krzysztof Kieślowski moved from producing documentaries to cinematic fiction because he had become increasingly phobic about the vampiric nature of filming the authentic emotions of people in real-life situations.

Žižek argues: 'It was precisely a fidelity to the Real that compelled Kieślowski to abandon documentary realism – at some point, one encounters something more Real than reality itself' (*Real Tears*: 71); and 'at the most radical level, one can portray the Real of subjective experience only in the guise of a fiction' (*Parallax*: 30), or, as Kieślowski himself puts it: 'Not everything can be described. That's the documentary's great problem. It catches itself as if in its own trap' (*Real Tears*: 72). The soubriquet *reality TV* thus describes an essentially self-defeating project. A central component of reality as it is directly experienced involves such abstract, non-filmable, but hugely influential emotions as desire. Desire, by its very nature, cannot be satisfied because it then ceases to be desire. In keeping with Žižek's observation that a word can change everything, it moves from a being a dynamic relational *situation* to tensionless *satiation*. The *situation of desire* is thus that a directly felt emotion is paradoxically dependent upon its non-realization, its failure to achieve a camera-friendly resolution – known in the desire-exterminating zone of pornography as the 'money shot'. There is a further structural relationship between desire and drive. When desire is exchanged for enjoyment of the failure to achieve satisfaction, drive is the result. Because desire is structured by its relation *to* the big Other, rather than being found *within* the big Other, the advent of the Big Brother TV franchise represents an over-compensatory reaction to the gaps and absences that structure social reality. Its on-going search for explicit revelation represents an unreflexive drive to capture the essentially unobtainable Real.

Žižek dismisses the notion that a neutral reality can be uncovered by objective revelation: 'A certain surplus effect is thus generated which cannot simply be cancelled through "demystification": it is not enough to display the mechanism behind the frame, the stage effect within the frame acquires an autonomy of its own . . .' (*Parallax*: 29). The manner in which reality TV fails its own eponymous aim bears out Žižek's diagnosis. The fact that 'the frame acquires an autonomy of its own' is reflected not only in the spate of an additional level of media formats designed to comment upon the original reality TV content (dedicated supplementary programmes like the UK's *Big Brother's Little Brother*) but also in the adoption of reality TV methods by traditionally 'serious' news programmes (see Taylor and Harris 2005). Žižek uses the example of a painting to develop this point. The painting's frame is supplemented by the way in which our perception of paintings is framed in additional, less literal ways. Thus, there is also a frame in terms of the way in which the content of the painting has been structured to create its overall effect and there is the frame created by the various cultural expectations with which we might approach it – the genre, the physical setting, the dominant artistic conventions, etc. – so that:

> The frame is always-already redoubled: the frame within 'reality' is always linked to another frame enframing

'reality' itself. Once introduced, the gap between reality and appearance is thus immediately complicated, reflected-into-itself: once we get a glimpse, through the Frame, of the Other Dimension, reality itself turns into appearance. In other words, things do not simply appear, they *appear to appear*. (*Parallax*: 29)

Whilst this analysis of appearance may 'appear' unduly eso-teric and theoretical, the point is that it is precisely theory, rather than an ever-more explicit quest for reality, that enables us to gain a perspective upon the ideological under-pinnings of the media's doomed quest to capture reality. From a Žižekian perspective, it is no coincidence that this attempt has been accompanied in the financial world by, to repeat Žižek's evocative description, 'the mad, self-enhancing circulation of capital, whose solipsistic path of parthenogen-esis reaches its apogee in today's meta-reflexive speculations on futures' (*Violence*: 10). Whilst a passion for reality domi-nates TV schedules, a noteworthy feature of the commodity fetishism of advanced capitalism is the paradoxically sophis-ticated way in which it only appears to work (few seriously believe that such abstract forms as financial derivatives have an intrinsically valuable substance). In practice, the severity of periodic financial crises underlines the extent of the self-deception involved: a capitalist system that prides itself upon its non-idealistic, pragmatic values actively requires a mass suspension of disbelief in order to function.

CONCLUSION

Today ... this 'No trespass!' is increasingly undermined: recall recent attempts to combine the 'serious' narrative cinema with the 'hardcore' depiction of sex, i.e., to include in a 'serious' film sex scenes which are played for the real

(we see the erect penis, fellatio, up to actual penetration).
. . . And I am tempted to suggest that the rise of 'reality TV'
in its different guises, from 'docusoaps' to *Survival* com-
petitor shows, relies on the same trend to obfuscate the line
that separates fiction from reality. Which ideological coordinates underlie this trend? (*Borrowed Kettle*: 146–7; 2004b
website)

We have seen in this chapter how Žižek's Lacanian approach
to the media tackles head-on the interlocked nature of the
big Other's role as a structuring relationship between the
contingent phenomenological experience of society and
individual subjectivity. Žižek's use of such Lacanian notions
as the big Other and the ontological triad of the Real, the
Imaginary, and the Symbolic demonstrates the way in which
our common-sense notions of reality fail to account adequately for the role played in our direct experience of life
by the impact of undoubtedly immaterial, but no less determining, gaps, voids, and absences. Fantasies (and the various
libidinal investments they serve to process) play a fundamental part in our individual and societal psyches. Despite
the decline in the overt symbolic efficiency of various meta-
narratives (the Church etc.), the big Other continues to exist
in very practical, albeit submerged, forms. To answer Žižek's
above rhetorical question, the ideological coordinates of the
reality TV trend are the extension of the disavowed cynicism
of commodity fetishism to wider, previously non-commercial
social discourse. The substratal ideology of reality TV shares
and contributes, at a cultural level, to the unbearable lightness of capitalist logic. Intelligent viewers may be deeply
cynical about reality TV's claims to realism, but nevertheless we allow its qualities of excessive personalization and
emotionality to symbolically decaffeinate traditionally more
substantial discourses. Whilst the big Other exists as an

evanescent structural relationship, *Big Brother* represents
a solid, definitively empirical, entity that can be profitably
captured for TV transmission.

Rather than interpret various communications technologies as neutral mediators, Žižek engages with their literal
screening effects, the profound role the media plays in the
dark heart of our self-constitution. Subjectivity is necessarily based upon a void, a cut, a separation from the otherwise
amorphous flux of reality from which the subject needs to be
separated to be a self-conscious subject at all. This paradox
of the subject depending upon an absence is furthered by the
symbolic castration we undergo that, despite the debilitating
connotation of the phrase, is what enables us to call a plant a
rose, a tree a chestnut tree, etc. – linguistic specificity at the
cost of communicational sensuality. The media exacerbates
this process yet, further, it enables our communicative and
symbolic potential but at the cost of potentially repressed
libidinal displacements and abjured fantasies that accompany
its screening of the fundamental traumas that ultimately
define us. The philosophical explanation of this ideological
effect can be found in Hegel's work, where

> the negation of a negation does not produce an unprob-
> lematic positive entity. Once we begin to consider the
> relationship between reality and its appearances new layers
> arise. For example, at the most basic level appearance intro-
> duces a gap between what something is and what it is not
> – the illusory aspect of appearance. At another level relating
> to the previously cited account of framing, 'things can also
> appear to just appear, concealing the fact that they are what
> they appear to be'. (*Parallax*: 30)

Reminiscent of Groucho Marx's quip, whilst defending a
man in court, that 'This man looks like an *idiot* and acts like

an *idiot*, yet all this should in no way deceive you – *he is an idiot!*' (*Looking Awry*: 73), Žižek via Hegel is describing the *mise-en-abyme* of self-conscious reflexivity that can occur within the society of the spectacle. This is the reason why Kieślowski rejected documentary-making in favour of fiction, because 'we get people playing themselves . . . the only way to depict people *beneath* their protective mask of playing is paradoxically, to make them *directly play a role*, i.e. to move into fiction. Fiction is more real than the social reality of playing roles' (*Real Tears*: 75). For Žižek: '. . . there is a domain of fantasmatic intimacy which is marked by a "No Trespass!" sign and should be approached only via fiction, if one is to avoid pornographic obscenity' (ibid.: 72).

The obscenity Žižek refers to has a two-fold relevance to today's mediascape. Literally, cinema becomes more pornographic in terms of the quantity of explicit sexual images and the breaking down of genre boundaries (e.g. the art-house cinematic pornography of *Baise-moi* [Virginie Despentes and Coralie Trinh Thi 2000] and *Intimacy* [Patrice Chéreau 2001], etc.). The obscenity also, however, refers to other forms of non-sexual intimacy, so that discussions of whether sex is taking place between contestants on reality TV shows merge seamlessly with the precise nature of what happened in the Oval Office with Monica Lewinsky and the precise shape of Bill Clinton's penis. Despite the manifest talk of erections, 'the price we pay for the fact "everything is discourse" is that discourse becomes *impotent* in the face of the most common idiotic reality' (*Real Tears*: 75–6). In such a climate, Simon Cowell is able to propose a 'Political X-Factor' (see Wintour 2009). Substantive political concepts are supplanted by the media's conceptually stultifying privileging of immediacy's dumb thing-ness – the commodified corollary of Roquentin's tree, the sublime objectification of ideology.

4

UNDERSTANDING MEDIA
The Sublime Objectification of Ideology

INTRODUCTION: THE UNCANNY FORM OF IDEOLOGY

... 'the medium is the message' because it is the medium that shapes and controls the scale and form of human association and action. The content or uses of such media are as diverse as they are ineffectual ... it is only too typical that the 'content' of any medium blinds us to the character of the medium .... (McLuhan 1995 [1964]: 9)

The uncanny, like charity, begins at home. (Haughton in Freud 2003 [1899–1919]: xlii)

McLuhan's above emphasis upon the crucial importance of recognizing the form/content relationship for understanding how the media works, resonates with Žižek's similar emphasis upon the way in which contemporary ideology tends to achieve its effects *through* its mode of delivery rather than its explicit content – the previously encountered wheelbarrow of ideology. Žižek's adaptation of the psychoanalytical method for interpreting the mediascape challenges his readers to look beyond the manifest meaning of our cultural products to uncover their latent significance. But to understand Žižek's approach properly requires avoiding the common misunderstanding of both Freudian dream theory and Marxian commodity theory. The latent meaning hidden in a dream/commodity cannot be simply deduced from the manifest meaning of the dream/commodity's specific imagery/properties. The significant meaning that needs to be considered is the very mode by which the latent is expressed *via* the manifest: 'In both cases the point is to avoid the properly fetishistic fascination of the "content" supposedly hidden behind the form: the "secret" to be unveiled through analysis is not the content hidden by the form ... but, on the contrary, *the "secret" of this form itself* (*Sublime Object*: 11). In terms of media, as McLuhan points out, the medium is not only the message but the m*a*ssage.

A typical Žižekian joke neatly illustrates his McLuhanite commitment to the idea that 'truth is not one perspective, "the true one," against the other, illusory one; it only occurs in the very *passage* from one to another perspective' (*Organs*: 62). There are three friends talking in a bar:

> ... the first one says, 'A horrible thing happened to me. At my travel agency, I wanted to say "A ticket to Pittsburgh" and I said "A ticket to Tittsburgh!"' The second one replies, 'That's nothing. At breakfast, I wanted to say to my wife "Could you pass the sugar, honey?" and what I said was "You dirty bitch, you ruined my entire life!"' The third one concludes, 'Wait till you hear what happened to me. After gathering the courage all night, I decided to say to my wife at breakfast exactly what you said to yours, and

I ended up saying 'Could you pass me the sugar, honey?'
(ibid.: 61)

Thus, Žižek takes us from a non-threatening, humorous, standard version of a Freudian slip (Tittsburgh), to
the intrusion of a traumatic emotional truth at the heart of
everyday normality. He helps us to see that the most traumatic situation is actually not the emotional outburst of the
second friend, but a moment in which nothing of substance
is said. However, in that non-utterance resides all manner of
psychologically destructive forces. The truly disconcerting
aspect of this insight is that, again *contra* King Lear, much
will come of saying nothing. The seemingly peaceful breakfast table in the above example is akin, in movie terms, to
the opening scene of David Lynch's film *Blue Velvet* (1986),
where the surface-level normality of a manicured suburban
lawn is shown through Lynch's worm's-eye view to belie
chthonic depths of teeming sliminess.

Žižek is particularly adept at detecting the wheelbarrow in
which ideology trundles past our noses owing to his methodological predilection for uncovering '*das Unheimliche*, the
uncanny, which is linked not, as some believed, to all sorts
of irruptions from the unconscious, but rather to an imbal-
ance that arises in the fantasy when it decomposes, crossing
the limits originally assigned to it . . .' (Lacan et al. 1977:
22). To gain theoretical distance from the confoundingly
familiar, psychoanalysis uses the German term *unheimlich*,
which, although normally translated as 'uncanny', literally
means 'unhomely'. The incongruity that fuels our sense of
the *uncanny* comes from a specific form of unease that affects
us precisely because we witness the *homely* but seen from a
disturbingly different perspective. As Haughton so pithily
expresses it earlier, the psychoanalytical attitude allows us
to look afresh at what might otherwise become excessively

naturalized and immune to critique – it constitutes a method for delineating what Freud termed 'the psychopathology of everyday life' (2001b [1901]).

This focus upon the mundane has been present from the very beginning of psychoanalysis; thus, in the prefatory comments to his first major case history, Dora (Ida Bauer), Freud justifies his publication of otherwise confidential patient information by asserting that 'she will learn nothing from it that she does not already know' (Freud 2001c [1901–5]: 9), and elsewhere he recounts how his patients frequently responded to his analyses with comments like: 'As a matter of fact I've always known it; only I've never thought of it' (cited in Thompson 1994: 192). Žižek takes this psychoanalytical familiarity with familiarity from the individual therapeutic encounter and extends it to the wider social environment of today's mediascape. This enables him to uncover the full implications of the uncanny whilst sidestepping the limitations of the positions adopted by the three friends talking in the bar.

- Friend 1 – unable to see the deeper significance of an 'innocent' slip of the tongue. From a Freudian perspective, there is no such thing as a pure accident, or in other words, 'a Freudian slip is when you say one thing but mean your mother' (Anon).
- Friend 2 – unable to communicate non-traumatically.
- Friend 3 – unable to communicate his sense of trauma and is consequently fated to lead a life entrapped in bad faith.

Through his 'patient ideologico-critical work' Žižek enables us to recognize and traverse the passage between these three registers so that we can see the real strangeness of the otherwise unremarkable. Characteristic of Žižek's media analysis and its emphasis upon the passage between form and content is this manner in which what seemed to be normal and un-threatening is actually pregnant with significance – the equivalent of what is really happening at the breakfast table. In order to gain conceptual purchase and re-problematize the very practical brazenness of today's mediated ideology, the form of Žižek's simultaneously entertaining and deeply serious, trauma-based philosophical-pyschoanalytical insights combines with their theoretical content to represent a working example of the recursive form/content relationship that his theory is designed to address. This innovative method is needed because, on a day-to-day basis, a number of filters prevent us from recognizing the deeply ideological nature of our most familiar experiences – *the impossible position of enunication.*

THE IMPOSSIBLE POSITION OF ENUNCIATION AND THE DESUBLIMATION OF IDEOLOGY

In one of Freud's letters, he tells a joke about a newly married man who when asked how beautiful his wife looks replied:

'I personally don't like her, but that's a matter of taste.' . . . by providing this answer, the subject pretends to assume the standpoint of universality from which 'to be likeable' appears as an idiosyncrasy, as a contingent 'pathological' feature which, as such, is not to be taken into consideration. The joke therefore relies on the impossible/untenable position of enunciation of the newly married: from this position, marriage appears as an act which belongs to the domain of universal symbolic determinations and should as such be independent of personal idiosyncrasies – as if the very notion of marriage does not involve precisely the 'pathological' fact of liking a particular person for no

particular rational reason. (*Indivisible Remainder*: 198, 199;
1997b website)

The impossible quality of this position of enunciation comes
from the fact that the newly-wed is saying something that
only appears so bizarre because of the degree to which the
'normal' response we expect from someone in his position
involves routinely uncredited levels of irrationality. Marriage
requires a degree of emotional commitment that only appears
'normal' when made from a position sustained by public/
legal/mutual recognition of the relationship. The *impossible
position of enunciation* of the newly-wed who is nevertheless
objective about his wife's attractiveness is thus an impossible
position, not because of the validity of its truth content, but
because a powerful set of both cultural and individual expectations and conventions makes it structurally impossible for
the groom to voice this opinion beyond a marriage of con-
venience (e.g. to obtain a Green Card). Arguably, the reason
behind the success of Žižek's breakthrough book *The Sublime
Object of Ideology* (1989) is that although it is, at first glance,
idiosyncratic and unfamiliar, it recasts Marx via Kant and
Lacan in order to uncover the uncanniness of the otherwise
prosaic. Žižek's analysis enables the reader to see how the
reality of mediated life is replete with impossible positions of
enunciation, positions that, despite being right in front of us,
we still manage to recognize only when they are pointed out.

The most common understanding of Kant's notion of the
sublime is based upon the feeling of wonderment the human
mind feels when confronted with an overwhelming natural
phenomenon like a hurricane or a physical entity as vast as
the Grand Canyon. What makes this notion of the sublime
a useful concept for analysing the ideological function of the
media is the way in which the sublime experience, whilst
appearing to represent the mind being overpowered by

Nature's might, in practice, serves to reinforce our privileged sense of human reason as something capable of maintaining its independence from that power. A sublime episode is ultimately a cerebral one: we manage to transmute the feeling into an aesthetic experience so that we are not overwhelmed by the scale or force of what confronts us. Žižek recalibrates this notion of the sublime to demonstrate how the contemporary media system comes to act as a sublime system of ideology but in the reverse manner to the disorientating power of a natural phenomenon. Rather than inspiring irrational awe, the media system achieves its ideological effects by acting as the cultural wallpaper to our lives, a process of desublimation. In this regard, Žižek says:

> One should recall here the ultimate lesson of Lacan concerning sublimation: in a way, true sublimation is *exactly the same* as desublimation. Let's take a love relationship: 'sublime' is not the cold elevated figure of the Lady who had to remain beyond our reach – if she were to step down from her pedestal, she would turn into a repulsive hag. 'Sublime' is the magic *combination* of the two dimensions, when the sublime dimension transpires through the utmost common details of everyday shared life – the 'sublime' moment of the love life occurs when the magic dimension transpires even in common everyday acts like washing the dishes or cleaning the apartment. (In this precise sense, sublimation is to be opposed to idealization.) (*On Belief*: 41)

Despite our familiarity with Marshall McLuhan's adage 'the medium is the message', in practice we tend to consume media content with the presumption that it represents relatively objective, neutral news reporting, or overtly fictional, ideology-free formats which can be enjoyed harmlessly. The ensuing result is that an 'impossible position of enunciation characterizes the contemporary cynical attitude: in it, ideology can lay its cards on the table, reveal the secret of its functioning, and still continue to function' (*Indivisible Remainder*: 200; 1997b website). The naturalized nature of media ideology means that the critical equivalent of the outspoken newly-wed within media discourse is profoundly lacking. Media discourse is routinely informed by non-rational elements the actual logical oddness of which we pass over because of their familiar, matter-of-fact status. From a Žižekian perspective, there are three main modes of ideological desublimation: the ignorant ideologue, the cynical knave/ideologue, and the non-ideological ideologue.

Mode 1: The Ignorant Ideologue – the Philanthropic Racist

A Louisiana justice of the peace said he refused to issue a marriage license to an interracial couple out of concern for any children the couple might have. Keith Bardwell, justice of the peace in Tangipahoa Parish, says it is his experience that most interracial marriages do not last long.

'I'm not a racist. I just don't believe in mixing the races that way,' Bardwell told the Associated Press on Thursday. 'I have piles and piles of black friends. They come to my home, I marry them, they use my bathroom. I treat them just like everyone else.' (Huffington Post 2009)

There are two key forms of contradiction here: Justice Bardwell justifies acting in a racist fashion in order to prevent future racism; and the inadvertent proof of his racist beliefs is contained within the very form his denial takes – 'they use my bathroom'. For this denial to be uttered at all requires an *a priori* consideration of whether it is legitimate for black people to use the bathroom of a white person – a consideration that is racist in its very essence. Mode 1 is hence a relatively unsophisticated form of ideological desublimation. Although the racist thought is submerged within a superficially non-racist sentiment, the clumsiness of the desublimation allows for the enunciator to be confronted with the difficult-to-avoid implications of his own statement. Extending this type of ideology to society at large, whether those in power manage to deflect the accusation or not, they can at least be accused of wrongdoing from a recognizably political perspective.

Mode 2: The cynical knave/ideologue and the knowing wink[1]

Emblematic of *je sais bien, mais quand même*, Mode 2 is evident in the previously cited incident from Chapter 1 in which Peter Mandelson was accused of calling News International executives 'chumps' – an incident that raises several ideological issues:

(a) *The media's enervation of politics.* Amidst the brief controversy over Mandelson's slip of the tongue, there was little, if any, recognition of the political irony/inappropriateness of a key figure in a formerly socialist party being so angry for failing to obtain the support of *The Sun*, the biggest-selling right-wing tabloid newspaper in the UK. Whilst it is still possible to point to this contradiction, the political substance of the charge has become increasingly anachronistic. The deliberate, strategic, self-styled New Labour courting of capitalist interests means that complaints from a traditionally socialist perspective are likely to be dismissed with a call 'to get real'.

(b) *Collective bad faith – the system can function even if it makes fun of itself.* Mandelson's defence that he used the word 'chump' simultaneously both depends upon and produces a corresponding level of bad faith in his audience. An ethically based criticism of his actions is supplanted by admiration at the verbal dexterity with which he avoids responsibility for the true import of the enunciation. The Mandelson incident demonstrates how plausible deniability has become a naturalized feature of the media system. In relation to the presidencies of both Silvio Berlusconi and Nicolas Sarkozy, for example, Žižek claims that today's mass-mediated politics represents a reversal from traditional political culture. Today, the obscenity is on the surface whilst deep belief (e.g. ethical censure) only survives at the personal level. By contrast, in the past, public rhetoric involved the evocation of socially binding ethical and political values, even if those values were regularly traduced behind the scenes by individually cynical politicians. This demonstrates Arendt's point that once a people have proved themselves to be gullible or cynical enough to be deceived, even when 'they were given irrefutable proof of their falsehood, they would take refuge in cynicism; instead of deserting the leaders who had lied to them, they would protest that they had known all along that the statement was a lie and would admire the leaders for their superior tactical cleverness' (Arendt 1994 [1951]: 382).

(c) *Transgression and reinforcement of the system are not mutually exclusive.* Instead of distancing him from the media system's norms, Mandelson's initial obscenity ultimately served to bind him closer to them. Rather than being threatened, the media system needs the rejuvenating effect of foreclosed opposition – its constitutive transgression. This explains how formerly rebellious musicians come to transgress their initial transgression. They become co-opted back into the system they formerly built their success upon opposing. On UK TV this takes the form of advertisements by Iggy Pop selling

Swiftcover car insurance and Johnny Rotten, the urban punk *bête-noire*, reduced to selling Country Life butter.

In mode 2, the political realm is etiolated. The very notion of a committed ethical/political stance seems fanciful in an age of institutionalized cynicism from both politicians and their audiences.

Mode 3: The Non-Ideological Ideologue and the Chocolate Laxative

In contrast to both modes 1 and 2, this is the background set of assumptions that are not consciously examined at all because they are so totally taken for granted. Ideology in mode 1 is overt: the judge is clearly racist. Mode 2 achieves its effects with at least partial recognition (prior to subsequent repression) of an ethical/political problem. The audience really knows that Peter Mandelson used possibly the most offensive Anglo-saxon swearword – its enjoyment of the situation is derived from the knowingness of the wink with which Mandelson denies culpability. Mode 3 is distinguished by the way in which it achieves its effects by naturalizing the particularity of a political situation so that the dialectical relationship between cause and effect is lost completely. This is achieved by the manner in which the media displaces inconsistent attitudes towards social antagonism on to a false, misleadingly simple problem/solution.

A concerning feature of mode 2's functional ability to hold contradictory attitudes at the same time is that, despite being dressed up in democratic trappings, it shares an element of the Fascist mentality: '"Fascism", in its ideology and practice, is nothing but a certain formal principle of distortion of social antagonism, a certain logic of its displacement by a combination and condensation of inconsistent attitudes'

(*Ticklish Subject*: 186). It is therefore complacent to relegate this ideological danger safely to an historical past. The friendly fascism of mass media relies upon the same basic process: it distorts the social antagonisms/contradictions that can still be noticed in mode 2 onto another plane where they become invisible through their excessive transparency. This is how world hunger and global structural economic inequalities are conflated with celebrity values in such media spectacles as Live Aid/Eight. These celebrity-led events represent stark large-scale examples of a type of phenomenon Žižek labels, after a product he encountered in America, 'the chocolate laxative'. Although perhaps of peristaltically questionable validity, the term nevertheless evocatively describes the ideological process of manipulation in which the problem (the chocolate that causes the constipation) is sold as the solution (its laxative effects).

Whilst the racial bigotry exhibited in mode 1 exists independently of the media, Justice Bardwell's self-deluding, racist rationale foreshadows the directly mediated ideological operations involved in the other two modes. In mode 3, ideology comes to naturalize inconsistency to the point that it is no longer recognized as inconsistency – within Nazi Germany it was possible to quite like individual Jews but despise the race as a whole ('the Jew I know and like is not the same as the rest of *them*'). Inconsistency stops being an inconsistency when mere social ubiquity makes an attitude innately unproblematic. Hence today we stop recognizing the profound contradictions involved within celebrity-sponsored famine relief. Nazi Germany represents an extreme, horrendous extrapolation of what is, nevertheless, a primary mode of ideological efficacy in general. Through the tautological significance of the media spectacle, celebrity relief initiatives help to normalize the parallel existence and processing of two otherwise contradictory attitudes:

- A public sense of deep compassion at the sight of African famine.
- An unwillingness, derived from a chocolate laxative mindset, to confront the true causes of such famine. One is led to believe that famine is being eradicated by redirecting part of the revenue created from Western patterns of consumption towards the famine caused by that same consumerist mentality. Western shoppers who prop up the global economic system that denies the agricultural sectors of the developing world the opportunity to compete on a level playing field are granted the opportunity to solve the problems their system of commodity consumption has caused by . . . buying more music industry products. Rather than solving their bottom-line political and economic causes, perennial food shortages are transformed into equally perennial media spectacles.

In stark contrast to Hillary Clinton's anodyne 'It takes a Village' rhetoric, Žižek radically re-reads M. Night Shyamalan's film *The Village* (2004) as a dramatic portrayal of the ideological process whereby those most responsible for sustaining global economic iniquities are often presented by the media as the most ethically aware. *The Village* portrays an early American pioneer settlement in the Pennsylvanian woods where the villagers live in a state of fearful accommodation with a creature that inhabits the surrounding woods. The creature does not enter the village and the people do not venture into the woods. It is only towards the end of the film that the viewer is shown that the village elders are actually social refugees from the contemporary world. Having suffered various misfortunes and crimes, they have retreated to this isolated village to raise children in ignorance of the outside world. Žižek suggests that '[i]n a proto-Hegelian way, the external threat the community is fighting is its own inherent essence' (*Violence*: 23). He extends this speculation, applying it to our current conceptualizations of 'ethical consumption'. Supposedly well-intentioned attempts to escape a socially and ecologically harmful capitalist dynamic are merely disguised forms of that very system in action:

> What if the true evil of our societies is not their capitalist dynamics as such, but our attempts to extricate themselves from them – all the while profiting. . . . The exemplary figures of evil today are not ordinary consumers who pollute the environment and live in a violent world of disintegrating social links, but those who, while fully engaged in creating conditions for such universal devastation and pollution, buy their way out of their own activity . . . . (*Violence*: 23; undated website)

Žižek's dialectical shift of perspective from Hegel to Hollywood and back again brings to the fore the hypocrisy of those within the capitalist media who exacerbate the problems created by the global economic system whilst subjectively appearing to be part of its solution. Through the media's use of individual figures like George Soros and Bob Geldof, feel-good philanthropy is promoted at the expense of the shame-induced fundamental political and economic reform actually needed in order to achieve effective long-term solutions to such contradictions as the co-existence of net world food surpluses and persistent regional famine. In 2009, the now *Sir* Bob Geldof (amongst other celebrities) appeared in a series of TV adverts promoting the UK Government-sponsored financial investment product Premium Bonds. Rather than fundamentally contradicting Geldof's other media appeals to eradicate world famine, from a Žižekian perspective, it is the flip-side of the same ideological coin.

THE MEDIA MESSAGE OF FASCIST UNIVERSAL HEALTHCARE

The previously discussed inadvertent proof of Justice Bardwell's racist beliefs contained within his very denial can be interpreted as an *(un)knowing wink* – the racist attitude is successfully conveyed whether you believe it was consciously expressed or not, or whether the offending party meant to say it or not. Typically, the media serves as an overarching sublime object/process of ideology in which mode 1's most explicitly ideological nature is manipulated and obscured within the other two modes. The heated nature of the 2009–10 media debates about the reform of the US system of healthcare, in which proponents of healthcare reform were called Nazis, can be seen as an emotional, fearful response to the ideological threat posed by recognition of a competing sublime object of ideology to those that normally appear in the service of more conservative politics. Its opponents realized that universal entitlement to medical services is based upon a fundamentally different set of political assumptions. As a politically sublime system of ideology, the 'socialized medicine' well established in Europe for decades threatened to answer a fundamental social antagonism: 30 million uninsured Americans excluded from unproblematic access to medical services. Conservative political fear of this successful working embodiment of a socialist conception of a 'public good' displays the three modes of ideology previously encountered:

The ignorant ideologue. This category is revealed in the mode of disclosure. It is reflected in the inherent contradiction of the 'philanthropic' advocate of non-insurance. Concern about practical access to basic healthcare is sublimated into a more pressing concern that citizens remain 'free' from the dangers that accompany the receipt of socialized healthcare.

The cynical ideologue and the knowing wink. Of course we know that President Obama's plan was not Nazi and of course there will not really be 'death panels', but even so ... it makes a provocative news story complete with protestors' banners and T-shirts bearing Nazi symbols. The febrile nature of these Nazi accusations indicates a strength of feeling that draws upon the right wing's recognition of the power of sublime objects of ideology that usually work in its favour (e.g. the phantasmatic 'invisible hand' of the market mechanism) and the disproportionate unease caused by this recognition of universal healthcare as 'the one that got away'. The 'fascist' charges levelled against Obama were projections of the conservative position's own inconsistency – it is better that poor Americans are 'free' from healthcare rather than being 'enslaved' to the tyranny of basic medical entitlements.

The non-ideological ideologue. Purportedly, it's not a question of ideology but the neutral element of 'choice'. To counter this potential power of the sublime object of healthcare, the sublime rhetoric of choice is used:

> ... where the Republican critique of healthcare plan really works is by appealing to this basic gut notion of freedom of choice. And I think this is a problem; we have to confront it. But first we should make it clear that in order to exercise the freedom of choice – one has to repeat this again and again ... to really exercise this, an extremely complex network of social, legal regulations, even, I would say, ethical rules, which are somehow accepted, and so on ... have to be here. In other words, often less choice, at least less

public choice, at a certain level means more choice at a different level. (Žižek 2009a video interview)

Here Žižek tackles head-on the supposedly non-ideological, uncontroversial advocacy of 'free choice' in the guise of the misleadingly loaded question 'who could be against the desirability of choice?' Against capitalist media's tendency to produce a one-dimensional portrayal of choice as an unquestionable good, Žižek emphasizes how this characterization clouds the indispensable context from which choice derives its substance: the minimum standards of basic social infrastructure that need to exist before truly meaningful free choice is possible. Interestingly, the financial crisis that immediately preceded these vociferous objections to 'socialist healthcare' in America created an impossible position of enunciation that was difficult for US media advocates of the free market to acknowledge. They were faced with the awkward situation in which the free-choice tenet of the capitalist banking system was ultimately guaranteed by taxpayers' funding, which in absolute monetary terms now makes the United States one of the largest socialist states in the world.

THE SILENCE OF THE LAMBS, THE IGNORANCE OF THE CHICKEN, AND THE CYNICISM OF FORREST GUMP AND THE KUNG FU PANDA

That is the true stake of psychoanalytic treatment: it is not enough to convince the patient of the unconscious truth of his symptoms; the Unconscious itself must be induced to accept this truth. This is where Hannibal Lecter himself, that proto-Lacanian, was wrong: it is not the silence of the lambs but the ignorance of the chicken that is the subject's true traumatic core. (*Parallax*: 351)

The anecdote of the madman and the grain of corn (see Chapter 1) is an important one for the way in which it illustrates how Žižek's work on belief and ideology brings together individual psychology and wider social institutions. Lacan uses *'les non-dupes errent'* as a homophonic phrase for *'le nom de père'* (the name of the Father – a source of symbolic authority), to convey the crucial insight that those who claim not to be duped by the practical performative efficiency of symbolic fictions are really those most deeply mired in error. In terms of the anecdote, the madman is not merely mad, but more precisely psychotic – the condition in which one is no longer able to access metaphorical meaning. The psychotic's mind is destabilized as the symbolic order becomes disturbingly literal.[2] For the madman to be genuinely fearful of being eaten by the chicken requires that he has lost his sense of the necessary distance between material reality and the symbolic order. The madman after treatment comes to know at a rational level that he is no longer a grain of corn, yet he is still concerned that the chicken (the big Other) is not aware of this fact. By contrast, the issue for the contemporary cynic is not that the big Other is interpreted too literally, but rather that it is denied. This creates a new set of problems as, once again, what is denied and repressed tends to reappear elsewhere so that, as we have seen, the decline in belief in the big Other has produced such compensatory developments as reality TV.

In 'primitive' cultures, belief was naturally embodied in various rites and objects, for example the totem pole in North America. The mistake made by modern thinkers, Žižek argues, was to think that this form of belief was directly held: 'Premodern societies did not believe directly, but through distance. ... Enlightenment critics misread "primitive" myths – they first took the notion that a tribe originated from a fish or a bird as a literal direct belief, then rejected it as stupid, "fetishist," naïvety. They thereby imposed their own notion of belief on the "primitivized" Other' (*Puppet*: 6). Žižek suggests that postmodern forms of belief have further exacerbated this Enlightenment misreading. Demonstrating the crass inaccuracy of the Žižek-as-postmodernist trope, Žižek's analysis of mediated belief provides the basis of his distinctly non-relativist analysis of the profoundly ideological nature of today's media system. 'Primitive' societies' beliefs used objects and rituals, but *at a distance*: 'According to a well-known anthropological anecdote, the "primitives" to whom certain "superstitious beliefs" were attributed, when directly asked about them, answered that "some people believe", immediately displacing their belief, transferring it onto another' (Žižek 1998 website). By contrast, the postmodernist also claims distance from direct belief, but, and this is the crucial distinction, because of her need to adopt a cynical attitude to the very notion of belief, she is less able than the so-called 'primitive' to take conscious responsibility for its displaced nature. Despite her disavowals, the belief still functions, because in postmodern belief we *pretend to pretend to believe*. Žižek's theoretical insight is that, whereas 'primitive' cultures develop working modes of symoblism/ideology embodied in social rituals and objects, if pushed, their members retain the ability to maintain a healthy sceptical distance towards those practices.

Primitives act at a social level as if they believe, but at an individual level they may in fact demur; meanwhile, 'advanced' media consumers are part of a cynical zeitgeist but, as individuals, act with belief. Thus, rather than being evidence of the presence of unsophisticated fetishes, items such as totem poles in fact reveal a sophisticated familiarity with the self-generating power of belief and rituals (symbolic efficiency) and how they serve to bind the individual to society. By contrast, the postmodern person's typical affectation of distance through cynical detachment is more complicated than it at first appears:

> The most skeptical attitude, that of deconstruction, relies on the figure of an Other who 'really believes'; the post-modern need for the permanent use of the devices of ironic distantiation (quotation marks etc.) betrays the underlying fear, that without these devices, belief would be direct and immediate – as if, if I were to say 'I love you' instead of the ironic 'As the poets would have put it, I love you,' this would entail a directly assumed belief that I love you – that is, as if a distance is not already operative in the direct statement 'I love you.' (*Puppet*: 6–7)

For primitives, whether symbols are believed in literally or not, their ability to bind the culture together through mutual active participation and shared responsibility remains effective. Symbols function by embodying a form in which an individual can achieve distance from direct belief – the totem pole does the work of belief – but that necessary distance is an organic part of the day-to-day social structure. Belief assumes much less organic forms in a contemporary society dominated by sublime media of ideology.

Two key examples Žižek repeatedly uses in his work to illustrate the complex nature of contemporary belief are the anecdote of the physicist Niels Bohr's superstitious use of a horse-shoe and the French philosopher Blaise Pascal, who pointed out that the mere act of engaging in a religious ritual like the Catholic mass generates belief largely irrespective of one's conscious decision-making:

> Niels Bohr ... provided the perfect example of how ... a fetishist disavowal of belief works in ideology: seeing a horse-shoe on his door, the surprised visitor said that he

doesn't believe in the superstition that it brings luck, to [which] Bohr snapped back: 'I also do not believe in it; I have it there because I was told that it works also if one does not believe in it.' What this paradox renders clear is the way a belief is a reflexive attitude: it is never a case of simply believing – one has to believe in belief itself . . . and Bohr just confronts us with the logical negative of this reflexivity (one can also NOT believe one's beliefs . . .).

At some point, Alcoholics Anonymous meet Pascal: 'Fake it until you make it . . .' . . . Pascal's 'Kneel down and you will believe!' has to be understood as involving a kind of self-referential causality: 'Kneel down and you will believe that you knelt down because you believed!' The second thing is that, in the 'normal' cynical functioning of ideology, belief is displaced onto another, onto a 'sub- ject supposed to believe,' so that the true logic is: 'Kneel down and you will thereby MAKE SOMEONE ELSE BELIEVE!' (Žižek 2005c website; *Parallax*: 353)

Žižek draws attention here to the self-referential nature and performative element of the symbolic efficiency involved in what may otherwise appear to be simply a basic act of belief. A common-sense understanding might suggest there is a simple causality: an individual has a personally held view or emotional attachment to an ultimately unprovable, abstract entity, whether that be God or the superstition of the lucky horse-shoe. Žižek opens up this understanding to show that belief has an interrelated individual and collective nature. Not only can performing rituals have a belief-generating capability independently of an individual's intentions, this effect can be transmitted to others in a contemporary medi- ated form of Durkheim's anthropologically informed notion of *collective effervescence*.

So far, Žižek's account of belief corresponds to the

primitive's experience of his symbolic culture – he may not believe it literally himself, but he goes along with it because it binds the tribe together. The particular significance of Žižek's analysis for the media's relationship to ideology resides in his insights into how belief-based rituals and objects function as mechanisms through which the otherwise traumatic nature of belief is desublimated:

> 'You believe too much, too directly? You find your belief too oppressing in its raw immediacy? Then kneel down, act as if you believe, and YOU WILL GET RID OF YOUR BELIEF – you will no longer have to believe yourself, your belief will already ex-sist objectified in your act of praying!' That is to say, what if one kneels down and prays not so much to regain one's own belief but, . . . the opposite, to GET RID of one's belief, of its over-proximity, to acquire a breathing space of a minimal distance towards it? To believe – to believe 'directly,' without the externalizing mediation of a ritual – is a heavy, oppressing, traumatic burden, which, through exerting a ritual, one has a chance of transferring it onto an Other . . . (Žižek 2005c website)

A key phrase here is 'minimal distance'. The defining feature of postmodern attitudes towards belief is that the attempt to create this distance by virtue of cynicism (e.g. the death of God and all meta-narratives – rather than the accommodation with belief practised within 'primitive' culture) proves ineffective at adequately externalizing the trauma that belief causes. The result is that the repressed ultimately returns. However, unlike the primitive's working compromise between public belief and individually held cynicism, we believe in ways we don't realize – *not because our beliefs are manipulated behind our backs but because the manipulation occurs in our full view, in a misleadingly naturalized manner.*

Counter-intuitive as it sounds, the notion of something being hidden by virtue of its very visibility is well recognized within literature. For example, in G.K. Chesterton's 'The Sign of the Broken Sword',[3] in order to cover up the murder of a fellow officer, a General deliberately engineers a costly battle because 'if a man had to hide a dead body, he would make a field of dead bodies to hide it in' (Chesterton 2004 [1911]). Similarly, in Edgar Allan Poe's 'The Purloined Letter' a much sought-after letter (one that is crucial to the extent that in the wrong hands it could cause an international incident and potentially war) is hidden by the diplomat who stole it, on his apartment's noticeboard, in clear sight of those searching for it (see Muller and Richardson 1988). Continuing in this vein, Žižek suggests that *Forest Gump* epitomizes the cultural manifestation of contemporary ideology's beguiling transparency in a fashion akin to how Argentina's economy minister once escaped through a crowd of protesters wearing a mask of himself, since '*a thing is its own best mask*' (*Parallax*: 28). In the contemporary mediascape, ideological processes are embodied in range of non-threatening cultural forms much more subtle in their effects than Althusser's notion of overtly Ideological State Apparatuses, for example:

> The ideological mystification of [*Forrest Gump*] resides in the fact that it presents Ideology at its purest as non-ideology, as extra-ideological good-natured participation in social life. . . . *Forrest Gump* reveals the secret of ideology (the fact that its successful functioning involves the stupidity of its subjects) in such an open way that, in different historical circumstances, it would undoubtedly have subversive effects; today, however, in the era of cynicism, ideology can afford to reveal the secret of its functioning (its constitutive idiocy, which the traditional, pre-cynical

ideology had to keep secret) without in the least affecting its efficiency. (*Indivisible Remainder*: 200; 1997b website)

Like *Forrest Gump*, the Dreamworks animated film *Kung Fu Panda* (John Stevenson and Mark Osborne 2008) illustrates 'the way beliefs function in our cynical society – the film is ideology at its embarrassing purest' (Žižek 2009b website).

This claim is based upon the way in which the film re-engineers the key Lacanian insight that, just as the big Other has no material existence, so the object cause of our desires, *objet a*, also does not exist in any directly material sense. However, whilst Lacan developed an intricate theory of the nonetheless profound contribution the immaterial *objet a* plays in the necessary fantasies we construct to manage our symbolic encounter with the Real, by contrast, *Kung Fu Panda*'s ideological message consists in the manner with which it combines cod ancient Chinese wisdom and cynical everyday quips in order to undermine the symbolic efficiency of *objet a*. Both the eponymous panda's father and his Kung Fu master tell him that the 'secret ingredient' of their famous soup and fighting method (respectively) are based merely upon the belief that they are special rather than any actual substantive content underpinning their specialness. According to Žižek:

> What unites them is the rejection of objet a, of the sublime object of passionate attachment – in the universe of *Kung Fu Panda*, there are only everyday common objects and needs, and the void beneath, all the rest is illusion. . . . In what, then, does the ideology of the film reside? Let us return to the key formula: 'There is no special ingredient. It's only you. To make something special you just have to believe it's special.' This formula renders the fetishist

disavowal (split) at its purest – its message is: 'I know very well there is no special ingredient, but I nonetheless believe in it (and act accordingly) . . .' Cynical denunciation (at the level of rational knowledge) is counteracted by a call to 'irrational' belief – and this is the most elementary formula of how ideology functions today. (Žižek 2009b website)

Despite the fact that postmodernity marks a moving on from modernity's *passion du réel*, its disclaimed beliefs have reappeared in a passion for reality TV and the *ideology of the reel* – the sublimely ideological Hollywood films like *Forrest Gump* that, as we have seen, achieve their effects in the guise of not being ideological. Žižek's analysis removes the fake alibi provided by only purportedly ironic consumption. Instead, at a time when recognition of the importance of symbolic fictions has been replaced by increasingly sophisticated technologically processed fictions, CGI, etc., he helps us take more direct responsibility for the role the media plays in *screening* our social fantasies.[4]

CONCLUSION: *MINORITY RAPPORT* AND THE MILLION DOLLAR NON-QUESTION

The predominant way of maintaining a distance towards the 'inhuman' Neighbor's intrusive proximity is politeness – but what is politeness? . . . A boy and a girl are saying goodbye late in the evening, in front of her house; hesitantly, he says: 'Would you mind if I come in with you for a coffee?', to which she replies: 'Sorry, not tonight, I have my period . . .' A polite version would be the one in which the girl says: 'Good news, my period is over – come up to my place!', to which the boy replies: 'Sorry, I am not in the mood for a cup of coffee right now . . .' (*Lost Causes*: 17)

Žižek's coffee-centred anecdote is reminiscent of a similar scenario in *Seinfeld*.[5] Awkwardly sitting in his car with his date as he drops her off home, the socially maladroit character George Costanza declines an invitation to go upstairs to her apartment for a coffee on the grounds that he doesn't like coffee – only to curse himself later for not realizing what his date *really* meant. As in the previously cited example of Field Marshal von Kluge whose chance to kill Hitler was stymied by an over-active sense of politeness (see Chapter 1), superficially only a rather bland social lubricant, civility actually acts as a powerful screening device for the potentially traumatic nature of various social encounters. Civility and politeness encode individual encounters with universal, socially determining notions and standards of behaviour. The media plays a privileged role in this context. The semantic tautology of the fact that media mediate and technological screens screen our social experience belies the crucial ideological significance of those tautologies. The point is not that such screening is somehow avoidable or illegitimate, but rather that contemporary ideology facilitates our failure to take full responsibility for the various literal and metaphorical screening and mediating functions assumed by our ubiquitous media screens.

This chapter's analysis of the various modes of ideology shows how the post-politics of mass media democracy, albeit in a much more media-savvy way, has surprising/worrying resonances with Justice Bardwell's philanthropic racism. His refusal of a marriage licence to a mixed-race couple appears in the form of a disavowal of racism through its reduction to the administration of social matters within the existing framework of liberal democratic discourse. It is not Justice Bardwell himself, *of course*, who wants to stop the couple getting married, but his liberal-inspired concern to protect the possible children from any union of racism (a potential plot for the movie *Minority Rapport*?). This is the sort of disingenuous sentiment that fosters racism whilst carefully remaining within a democratic, human rights, frame of reference. True politics for Žižek is 'something that *changes the very framework that determines how things work*' (*Ticklish Subject*: 199). The true political act for Justice Bardwell therefore would be to be eschew his defence made in bad faith and to be open with his racist views – he could then be opposed accordingly in a correspondingly true political act of opposition. Instead, Justice Bardwell represents an extreme case, the obscene underside, of a pervasive post-political technique that dominates contemporary media. Whichever oxymoronic figure under consideration, whether it be the philanthropic racist, the radically moderate politician, or the celebrity-aid-generator, the framework that determines how things really work is either left resolutely untouched, or made worse, by espousals of well-meaning acts and the best of intentions.

The internationally franchised TV show *The Secret Millionaire* illustrates this ideological screening process. In each episode, the millionaire is placed 'undercover', usually within a deprived inner-city neighbourhood. Over a period of days the millionaire, working under a suitable cover story to explain the presence of TV cameras, proceeds to scout out in the locale potentially deserving charitable organizations and individuals. The formula invariably shows the millionaires undergoing voyages of personal discovery in which their previous prejudices about poor people are typically undermined by the selfless acts of various social entrepreneurs. The ideological element of the programme functions seamlessly. Apart from the eponymous hero, the entrepreneurship on view does not take a financially rewarding form. What we see are various forms of social entrepreneurship from people who find themselves in adverse circumstances, but entrepreneurship is the value that is clearly still being celebrated. Perhaps of most significance is the programme's 'money shot' (in both literal and metaphorical senses of the term) when the millionaires are shown giving cheques to the various individuals and groups they have befriended. Footage rich in emotionality accompanies the philanthropic dispensing of largesse, but little if any consideration is paid to the veiled structural causes that have created a situation in which patently resourceful people are close to destitution whilst the benefactors, 'blessed' by their grateful recipients and their own newly recalibrated sense of good fortune, are able to grant what society at large up until this point has so signally failed to provide.

The real secret of *The Secret Millionaire* is not that the poor people don't know who the rich person in their midst is, nor is the true message the format's weakly desublimated ideology that, deep down, millionaires are just like you and me. Rather, the secret upon which the programme depends for its success is why two relatively simple questions are not asked by either the participants or the audience: what makes wealthy people still strive for yet more money and what sort of society allows such wealth disparity to exist in the first place? The conscious split between individual belief and social practice that the primitive makes in relation to the tribal fetish is taken an ideological stage further in the naturalized cynicism of the contemporary docudrama audience. We admire the politeness of 'the natives' encountered by the secret millionaire and we emote in accordance with the programmed values of the real-life philanthropy constructed as a spectacle. Both the politeness and the format, however, screen the primary political trauma that provides the spectacle's suitably down-at-heel recessionary urban backdrop. The primitive holds a perfectly rational belief in the overarching cultural efficacy of a symbolic order – an efficacy that exists whether specific aspects of that order's content are strictly rational themselves or not. He readily accepts that the symbolic order all societies require involves an element of fetishist disavowal in order to function smoothly. *The Secret Millionaire*'s audience, by contrast, exhibits a truly irrational belief. It unwittingly disavows through a fetishized screen more irrational than any totem pole the true secret it is watching: the systematic nature of mediated communication's symbolic violence to which we now turn.

5

THE MEDIA'S VIOLENCE

INTRODUCTION: MEDIATING VIOLENCE

More communication means at first above all more conflict.

(Peter Sloterdijk)[1]

Explicitly in *Violence* (2008) but implicitly throughout the rest of his *oeuvre*, Žižek problematizes the media's standard range of discourse. He explores the ideological processes involved in two main forms of violence in contemporary society: subjective and objective violence.

Subjective Violence

This is what we common-sensically understand by the notion of violence and is defined by Žižek as that which is 'performed by a clearly identifiable agent' (*Violence*: 1). In other words, subjective violence refers not to any notion of an excessively personal interpretation of what constitutes violence, but rather to violence that can easily be attributed to an individual source. In media terms, it can be seen in the dramatic forms of violence frequently shown on TV news programmes and the burgeoning number of 'embedded' journalistic reports, whether they are to be found in events like the Iraq war or the myriad reality TV shows thematically united by their devotion to violent encounters, for example various 'squad-car view' cop shows.

Objective Violence

Žižek subdivides objective violence into two parts:

(i) *Symbolic violence* – the basic form of violence 'that pertains to language as such' (*Violence*: 1). The cardinal philosophical point is that *all* communication has a violent element. The key political question rests in the *type* of violence that results. Thus, Baudrillard finds in the agonistic, threatening challenges laid down by anthropological forms of symbolic exchange a desirable form of communicational violence. Subtle nuances are contained within traditional rituals of gift-giving that produce a culture full of seductive ambiguities – to be contrasted with the pre-ordained, pre-enscribed cultural values transmitted within the exchange of commodities. At one level, the transmissions of this technologically mediated commodified order appear less symbolically violent than its more 'primitive' counterparts because less is demanded from the sender and recipient, but on another level it is steeped with violence of the following kind.

(ii) *Systemic violence* – 'the often catastrophic consequences of the smooth functioning of our economic and political systems' (*Violence*: 1). This concept refers to the predominantly unrecognized levels of force and repression that form a base-level, frequently dispersed, but nevertheless effective and powerful circumscription of social activity. The conventional notion of violence has been widened to include *de facto* economic coercion. For example, a cleaning worker on minimum wage may not be frog-marched out of the house each day to scrub toilets, but basic economic pressure acts as an effective force in its own right.

Žižek's concept of objective violence encapsulates his overall political and methodological approach – the striving to draw attention to those cultural elements that have profound effects but are largely invisible to the ideologically acclimatized eye:

> Objective violence is invisible since it sustains the very zero-level standard against which we perceive something as subjectively violent. Systemic violence is thus something like the notorious 'dark matter' of physics, the counterpart to an all-too-visible subjective violence. It may be invisible, but it has to be taken into account if one is to make sense of what otherwise seem to be 'irrational' explosions of subjective violence. (*Violence*: 2)

In a society of the spectacle, the invisibility of objective violence makes it media-unfriendly. Typically cursory attempts by TV news to provide historical context to its items are dominated by metronomically metonymic images. Complex cultural histories become inseparable in our mediated mind's eye with reductively familiar pictures: bombed-out downtown Beirut; emaciated African babies; Uzi-toting Israeli soldiers and *keffiyeh*-wearing Palestinian stone throwers. Thus the media propagates a fundamental form of mediated violence through its role as a sublime system of symbolic castration in which these explicit spectacles supplant sustained consideration of their primary causes – past and present. Just as the mundane violence that accompanied daily life under the pre-revolutionary *Ancien Régime* (the objective political cause of the subsequently subjectively experienced *Terror*) is systematically excluded from detailed consideration, so is the background level of global state-sponsored terror necessary for the continuation of 'normal' international politics by other means – *the War on Terror*.

OBSCENITY (IN)ACTION

A significant part of the media's symbolic violence consists in the systematically distorted and partial nature of its depiction of the historical role played by political violence. A spectacle-based agenda means that the relationship between violence and political progress is played down in preference for an airbrushing of the historical record and/or the depiction of political violence as an exclusively destructive force. In 1989 the French celebrated their revolution's Bicentennial, but as a TV spectacular complete with fireworks. To the extent that the violence of emblematic events like the French Revolution is considered, it tends to occur as sensationalized accounts of the Terror with little, if any, serious consideration of historical necessity and emancipatory success. This is exemplified by the BBC documentary *Terror! Robespierre and the French Revolution*.[2] Presented as a 'docudrama', the programme blended the opinions of historians, novelists, and cultural commentators (Žižek included) with dramatic re-enactments of key events in the first years of the Revolutionary government. Additional dramatic effect was achieved by using shots of the various contributors looking directly into the camera and voicing excerpts from Robespierre's speeches. Žižek functions in this programme as the *agent provocateur* who contradicts the programme's sustained depiction of the Terror as an unremittingly negative historical episode. Selectively edited for maximum shock-value, he is frequently juxtaposed with the British historian Simon Schama, who emotes heartfelt contempt for anyone who does not share his unreserved condemnation of the period's revolutionary excesses.

Amongst historians, estimates of the exact number of deaths directly attributable to the Terror vary. At the end of *Terror!*, the otherwise black screen is filled with the written statement that 55,000 people died between 1789 and 1793, which, in a crude calculus of historical deaths, appears as a relative anti-climax after the breathless tone of the pro-gramme's narrative. The symbolic violence typified by this TV portrayal consists of its systematic displacement of the terror suffered as a result of objective violence, an effect achieved through the media's disproportionate focus upon the subjective violence of the Terror. In *Living in the End Times* (2010) Žižek cites Mark Twain's *A Connecticut Yankee in King Arthur's Court* to emphasize what Schama et al. fail to recognize:

> There were two 'Reigns of Terror' if we would remem-ber it and consider it; the one wrought in hot passion, the other in heartless cold blood . . . our shudders are all for the 'horrors' of the minor Terror, the momentary Terror, so to speak, whereas, what is the horror of swift death by the axe compared with lifelong death from hunger, cold, insult, cruelty, and heartbreak? A city cemetery could contain the coffins filled by that brief Terror which we have all been so diligently taught to shiver at and mourn over; but all France could hardly contain the coffins filled by that older and real Terror, that unspeakably bitter and awful Terror, which none of us have been taught to see in its vastness or pity as it deserves. (Twain cited in *Living*: 387)

The historical and economic aspects of the grinding daily violence of the *Ancien Régime* are passed over in preference for more spectacle-friendly costumed historical re-enactments of the Terror's key dramatic moments. This ideological myopia occurs within contemporary settings too so that, in terms of on-going violence in the Democratic Republic of the Congo, the objective conditions of which were created by Western colonial exploitation, the media is unable to inform us to the *nearest million* the accumulated death toll from recent years: 'The Congo today has effectively re-emerged as a Conradean "heart of darkness". No one dares to confront it head on' (*Violence*: 2). A society of the spectacle that is otherwise predicated upon explicit revelation operates selective tunnel vision with regard to violence. Consider, as a cameo, the UK TV Channel 4 programme *Dispatches – The War Against Street Weapons*.[3] Presented by Cherie Blair, the wife of ex-British Prime Minister Tony Blair, the programme demonstrated no sense of irony about the glaring contrast to be made between the moral fervour informing its successful search for knives on the streets of Britain and the sang-froid of the presenter's husband when quizzed by the media about his failure to find weapons of mass destruction in Iraq.

The frequently obscene jokes that pepper Žižek's analysis thus need to be appreciated in their role of shocking Western media consumers from their uncritical accommodation with the objective violence committed in their name. Žižek's alleged tastelessness is put into the service of uncovering political obscenities that members of the established commentariat like Simon Schama are ill equipped to see – the disowned level of violence and harm visited upon others so that liberal democracies may function smoothly. In this regard, it is instructive to compare the highly dramatized sentiment of *Terror!* with calm discussions about the price to be paid for the 'non-violent' US/UK-sponsored UN sanctions against Iraq from 1990 to 2003. That these sanctions led to the deaths of hundreds of thousands of Iraqis, mostly children, is a charge that at least one leading Western government figure of the time failed to deny:

> *TV interviewer – Lesley Stahl:* We have heard that a half million children have died. I mean, that's more children than died in Hiroshima. And, you know, is the price worth it?
>
> *US Secretary of State – Madeleine Albright:* I think this is a very hard choice, but the price – we think the price is worth it.
>
> US Current Affairs Programme,
60 Minutes (5/12/96)[4]

Ironically, in the age of reality TV, the media nevertheless routinely engages in displacement activities with which to avoid confronting the uncomfortable reality of the hundreds of thousands of deaths that do not readily fit within its formats. By contrast, in the face of horrific levels of violence suffered by the Iraqi populace, both during and after the Allied invasion, and amidst a dearth of accurate statistics for the estimated hundreds of thousands of deaths, the British media's coverage of the invasion's aftermath was dominated for weeks by the undeniably tragic, but individual death of Dr David Kelly and the related resignation of a BBC reporter, Andrew Gilligan.[5]

THE MEDIA'S STANDARD OPERATING PROCEDURE

Photographs don't tell us who the real culprits might be. . . . They can also serve as a coverup, they can misdirect us.

... Photographs reveal and conceal, serve as [both] exposé and coverup. (Errol Morris)[6]

A standard operating procedure (SOP) of media discourse is the audience's carefully cultivated sense of shock – carefully cultivated in the sense that nominally traumatic images from around the world's trouble spots are presented to us in a viewing mode that is relatively detached and liable to ameliorate the images' potential to upset. Content is mediated not only literally by the cameras that purvey the images, but also by the overarching media format within which the pictures appear: the avuncular anchorman, the containment of items within discrete 'world news' segments, etc. Deviation from the media's SOP occurs when the traumatic content succeeds in breaking free from these reassuringly conventional settings. For example, as a number of commentators, including Žižek (Desert), have pointed out, one of the traumatic elements of the 9/11 images was the manner in which similar images had already been prefigured in both Hollywood representations and disaster zones elsewhere in the world. Images of 9/11 resonated so uncannily because they were simultaneously familiar and radically different; they intruded into our consciousness as recognizable images of what was only normally seen safely beyond US shores or in the movie theatre. At least a sense of the depth of the unreflexive emotional investment made in media SOP can be gained from observing the spontaneously irrational defensiveness and inconsistency exhibited towards those whose actions question it. Thus, whilst images of war victims from the Middle East are frequently shown on Western TV, reciprocal coverage of Allied deaths by al-Jazeera has met with angry Western denouncements.[7]

In this context, although nominally traumatic for their harrowing depiction of prisoner abuse, the true uncanniness

of the Abu Ghraib photographs stemmed from the resonance they evoked with the SOP of the same media and
wider society that purported to be shocked by their content.
Representing a form of 'shock in bad faith', the perverted
acting out by military personnel pictured in the photographs
was replicated by the media's act of publication without ade-
quate critical analysis of the pictures' profound parallels with
intrinsic Western cultural SOPs:

> The contrast between what happened latterly at Abu
> Ghraib and the 'standard' way prisoners were tortured
> during Saddam's regime is striking. Instead of the direct,
> brutal infliction of pain, the US soldiers focused on
> psychological humiliation. And instead of the secrecy prac-
> tised by Saddam, the US soldiers recorded the humiliation
> they inflicted, even including their own faces smiling stu-
> pidly as they posed behind the twisted naked bodies of the
> prisoners. When I first saw the notorious photograph of
> a prisoner wearing a black hood, electric wires attached
> to his limbs as he stood on a box in a ridiculous theat-
> rical pose, my reaction was that this must be a piece of
> performance art. The positions and costumes of the pris-
> oners suggest a theatrical staging, a tableau vivant, which
> cannot but call to mind the 'theatre of cruelty', Robert
> Mapplethorpe's photographs, scenes from David Lynch
> movies. This brings us to the crux of the matter. Anyone
> acquainted with the US way of life will have recognised
> in the photographs the obscene underside of US popular
> culture. You can find similar photographs in the US press
> whenever an initiation rite goes wrong in an army unit or
> on a high school campus and soldiers or students die or
> get injured in the course of performing a stunt, assuming a
> humiliating pose or undergoing sexual humiliation. (Žižek
> 2004c website)

Abu Ghraib's pornographically abusive photographs marked an unusually strong indication of how, looked at awry, the West's worst cultural excesses are merely the particularly dark flip-side of the same basic, perverted ideological process present amidst the humour as Comical Ali (Iraqi Information Minister Muhammad Saeed al-Sahaf) performed for the cameras. In the light of Abu Ghraib, there was a prescience to his claim about US troops: 'They are not in control of anything – they don't even control themselves!' (cited in ibid.). This ideological process was also evident in the overdetermined media staging of the 'Saving Private Lynch' incident. Here, the US media's pathological reliance upon spectacular revelation meant that awkward issues (like the fact that Iraqi medical personnel were actually prevented by US troops from safely returning Private Lynch shortly prior to her dramatically filmed 'rescue') were lost in the need to follow the Spielberg-infused SOP. To reiterate, 'the very fascination with the obscenity we are allowed to observe prevents us from *knowing what it is that we see*' (*Tragedy*: 8).

Further recent examples of the ideological role played by the media's SOP 'shock-tactics' include news agency accounts of the preternatural indifference exhibited by European holiday makers at the now regular sight of boatloads of desperate and dehydrated African economic migrants being brought into otherwise scenic harbours. Especially 'shocking' are the pictures of Italian sunbathers who failed to be discomforted enough by the nearby dead bodies of two Romany children to change their sunbathing spot.[8] In these sorts of instances, audiences are offered the opportunity to be shocked at other people's lack of shock. Žižek's theoretical analysis of the media's SOP provides an additional twist upon this twist. He encourages us to be shocked, not at other people's lack of shock, but at what we ourselves do not see in the very act of censuring other people's indifference. Expressed differently,

owing to the media's framing of events, we fail to see what it
is that we are really seeing. The callousness of the sunbathers
distracts us from seeing the viewer's own deep-rooted com-
plicity. We live within an economic system that, at the very
same time we are criticizing the moral myopia of European
holidaymakers, instantiates in its objective, callously violent
day-to-day functioning at a much more systemic level. Thus,
in September 2007, in what could perhaps be termed a 'bad
Samaritan law', the Italian judicial system charged seven
Tunisian fishermen with aiding and abetting illegal immigration. The fishermen's offence was the 'criminal' act of
coming to the aid of a boatload of drowning migrants that
included children and pregnant women. The incident yet
again provides a chilling illustration of Guy Debord's aphorism that '[i]n a world which *really is topsy-turvy*, the true is a
moment of the false' (Debord 1977 [1967]: N9), in so far as

> [t]he true object of the trial, it is suspected, is to dissuade
> fishermen from doing their duty. If so, it is likely to be
> successful. The fact that the fishermen have spent more
> than a month in custody sends a clear message to others
> like them.
>   Laura Boldrini, of the UN High Commission for
> Refugees, contrasts the behaviour of the Tunisians with that
> of other, unnamed fishermen reported to her who recently
> beat migrants attempting to get into their boat with sticks,
> forcing them into the water where several drowned. No
> action was taken against them. (Popham 2007)

On this occasion, the Maltese and Italian navies, apparently
under orders not to come to the aid of drowning migrants,
are the enforcers of objective violence. This is simply, but
all the more powerfully, underlined by the starkly contrasting humanitarian words of the Tunisian captain: 'I'm happy

about what I did . . . If I hadn't done it they would have died' (ibid.).

The invaluable contribution Žižek's critical reading offers to otherwise well-intentioned media reportage is a sense of the deeper needful libidinal investments at work in such basic media operations as the standardized production of shock. Outrage at ethnic violence, for example, can be viewed as a moral badge of the well-meaning liberal whose typical response is to call for more multicultural tolerance. Žižek's counter-intuitive point is that this call for more understanding is often disingenuous. There is an uncredited symbiotic relationship between the shocked 'ethical' call for greater understanding and the violence and horrors that sustain the moral position from which the ethical call is made. The ethos of multicultural tolerance requires ethnic conflict to justify its more humane and 'enlightened' perspective. Its tolerance is premised upon a much more powerful but foresworn intolerance towards an engaged analysis with the structural causes of ethnic conflict conveniently dismissed as tribal in origin. Morally informed shock is co-opted to preclude rather than enable effective understanding. Žižek repeatedly shows how the media's ideological effect occurs through its purportedly non-ideological SOP. Under the guise of exposing global trauma and injustice in spectacular detail, genuine consideration of the key political and economic causes is displaced. Žižek urges us to go beyond unproductive shock at other people's lack of shock.

As an illustration of the practical implications of the difference between objective and subjective violence, Žižek's analysis of ethnic conflict suggests the need for *more* not less distance between different cultures. A recognition of differences and the need to develop a working sense of civility and social distance with which to accommodate such differences is more important than the promotion of tolerance for its own sake. Again counter-intuitively, he argues that we need more, not less, hatred. The crucial difference being that the required hatred needs to be directed towards those systemic features that are the common enemy to all ethnic groups and the real causes of the economic inequalities that create the conditions that allow racism to prosper in the first place. Rather than misplaced shock at individual media reports that are frequently presented with almost exclusively visual emphasis and little or no political and economic context, Žižek's work constantly impresses upon us the need to consider the objective predictability of the media's SOP: the eternal return of ideology in the guise of non-ideological news reporting – faux objectivity that covers up objective violence.

Žižek suggests that the ideological corollary of our over-reliance upon mediated images is the naïvety of dominant social discourses (multiculturalism, identity politics, etc.) that propose such sentiments as 'a stranger is simply someone whose story we haven't heard yet'. He rejects these views, arguing that more consideration needs to be paid to the extent to which human communication is inescapably violent, rhetorically asking 'is one also ready to affirm that Hitler was an enemy because his story was not heard?' (*Violence*: 39). Sustained by the symbolic violence of the media's over-reliance upon subjective violence, objective violence continues to be overlooked. Notwithstanding the graphic images to which our society of the spectacle gives us constant access, and despite large numbers of media scholars devoted to fields of study like 'active audience studies', certain tragedies of staggering proportions, such as the new Conradian 'Heart of Darkness' in today's Congo, still manage to pass by as largely unreported non-events. Those traumatic intrusions into the mediated status quo that do occur therefore provide valuable insights into occasional breakdowns within the media's otherwise smooth ideological functioning.

THE TRAUMA OF COMMUNICATION: HURRICANE KATRINA AND THE SUBJECT SUPPOSED TO LOOT AND RAPE

Media coverage of Hurricane Katrina produced another vivid *tableau vivant*, this time one of racial inequality in the US, the image of which was subsequently exacerbated by racially profiled news reporting. White people taking food from a grocery store are pictured in a photograph released by the international news agency AFP with the accompanying description: 'Two residents wade through chest-deep water after *finding* bread and soda from a local grocery store after Hurricane Katrina came through the area in New Orleans . . .', whilst a very similar photograph of a black male in an Associated Press release is described thus: 'A young man walks through chest deep floodwater after *looting* a grocery store in New Orleans . . .' (emphasis added).[9] Amidst the slickly presented charity appeals for Katrina relief one broadcast in particular stood out, televised live East Coast by NBC on the evening of Friday, 2 September 2005.[10] The white North American comedian Mike Myers uses soft cadences to introduce the appeal, only to hand over to the African American rap artist Kanye West, who, his voice shaky with emotion, alludes to the two press agency photographs to criticize media portrayals of African American behaviour. Angrily, he points out that the country's military has been sent to the area with permission to shoot black people. Once Myers finishes his second part of the appeal (in a manner that inevitably appears muted compared to West's obvious animus), West concludes the segment by declaring 'George Bush doesn't care about black people!'

The factual substance of West's emotional outburst has been endorsed in retrospective analyses:

> Louisiana's governor at the time, Kathleen Blanco, announced as she dispatched National Guard troops: 'I have one message for these hoodlums: these troops know how to shoot and kill, and they are more than willing to do so if necessary, and I expect they will.' She and the city's mayor had called off the rescue efforts to focus on protecting private property – with lethal force if necessary. (Solnit 2009)

Solnit emphasizes how contemporaneous media accounts signally failed to recognize the humanity-affirming levels of support that (the disproportionately African American) victims showed to each other and then correspondingly failed to convey the alarming breakdown in morality amongst the much better situated (disproportionately white) law enforcement officials:

> Amusingly, the New Orleans Police Department stripped a Cadillac dealership of its cars, some of which were found as far away as Texas. Less amusingly, they shot a couple of unarmed – and, of course, black – family groups on the Danziger Bridge shortly after the storm in the only such incident to receive much press coverage. A middle-aged mother had her forearm blown off; a mentally disabled 40-year-old on his way to his brother's dental office was shot five times in the back and died, and a teenager was also killed. . . . Most people behave beautifully in disasters. . . . The majority in Katrina took care of each other, went to great lengths to rescue each other – including the 'cajun navy' of white guys with boats who entered the flooded city the day after the levees broke – and were generally humane

and resourceful. A minority that included the most powerful believed they were preventing barbarism while they
embodied it. (ibid.)

At both the macro- and micro-level, the Katrina aftermath
illustrates the traumatic Real that the act of communication
serves to process. At the macro-level, before on-the-scene
government press conferences could be arranged, the
world's TV and press had witnessed in stark, brutal terms
the inescapable race-based evidence of the socio-economic
inequality the hurricane had brought to the surface. At the
micro-level, within the normally controlled symbolic order
of the TV studio, the raw impression created by the juxtaposition of Mike Myers and Kanye West provided an unusual
insight into the extent to which the media's base-level functioning routinely excludes politically charged emotion and
struggles to contain its unscripted appearance – the violent
intrusion of heart-felt spontaneity into TV studios devoted
to the production of sanitized and commodified TV formats. The discomfort of the other presenters facing West
was marked and, despite the social distance from the Katrina
victims created by his wealth, his keenly felt racial empathy
('I hate the way they portray *us* in the media') demonstrated
an obvious strength of ethnic solidarity – a shared experience
accumulated in the face of objective historical discrimination.
West's heart-felt emotion clashed with the subjective, feel-
good philanthropic tenor that otherwise prevailed during
the TV appeal. West's critique was atypical in the US media
coverage, however. Whilst there was some critical reporting (see Thompson 2009), in general the US media failed
signally to recognize the US establishment's descent, during
Katrina's immediate aftermath, into its own Kurtzian heart
of darkness.

The psychological obverse of West's empathetic outburst

can be detected in the response of some white observers to the Katrina disaster. Replacing the psychoanalytical notion of 'The Subject Supposed to Know' with the Katrina-specific 'Subject Supposed to Loot and Rape', Žižek explores the manner in which we tend to embody our beliefs in uncritical, unreflexive tropes. The Katrina aftermath produced media accusations against African Americans that were invariably false. However, Žižek argues that *even if they had been true*, the additional question needs to be asked as to why some journalists/viewers/readers *wanted* them to be true. Irrespective of factual correctness, a desire to see an ethnic minority portrayed in a negative light conveys a more important, disturbing truth: a repressed level of emotional investment in wanting to be right about something that only confirms our deeper-rooted prejudices and biases. This can also be seen in reverse from by the differing reactions of African Americans and white Americans upon the announcement of the not-guilty verdict at the end of the original O.J. Simpson trial. The appropriate question to be raised here is not why did so many African Americans celebrate a non-guilty verdict even though, to the majority of the rest of the population, it appeared so incorrect, but rather, even if those African Americans were wrong, what made them want the 'wrong' verdict so badly? The seemingly 'unreasonable' African American celebratory response reflects a much deeper, political problem: repressed resentment about historical and on-going social injustices. It indicated, albeit again in reverse form, the validity of Žižek's notion of '*lying in the guise of truth*' (*Violence*: 85).

A similar illustration can be found in the UK press scandal over what eventually proved to be doctored photographs purporting to depict the abuse of Iraqi prisoners by British soldiers. Originally printed in the British national newspaper *The Mirror*, the pictures were soon proved to be fake and the newspaper's editor, Piers Morgan, was forced to resign. However, they represented 'telling the truth in the guise of a lie': they helped pave the way in the British polity for a franker discussion of the previously under-examined issue of British military abuses of power. To repeat for the final time Guy Debord's *aperçu* : 'In a world which *really is topsy-turvy*, the true is a moment of the false' (Debord 1977 [1967]: N9).

THE SYMBOLIC VIOLENCE OF MEDIATING ŽIŽEK

... an act always, by definition, involves a moment of externalization, self-objectivization, of the jump into the unknown. To 'pass to the act' means to assume the risk that what I am about to do will be inscribed into a framework whose contours elude my grasp, that it may set in motion an unforeseeable train of events, that it will acquire a meaning different from or even totally opposed to what I intended to accomplish – in short it means to assume one's role in the game of the 'cunning of reason'. (*Tarrying*: 31)

Although Žižek's willingness to appear in media outlets has contributed to accusations of buffoonery and clownishness, as indicated in the formerly encountered soubriquet 'The Marx Brother', it affirms Hegel's notion of a subject's authentic act. Žižek's self-subjection to the media's 'cunning of reason' enables him to uncover the media's ideological assumptions and symbolic violence not only through his scholarship, but also via inimitable media performances that problematize the act of communication being witnessed (form) as much as they conceptually enlighten the viewer (content). Perhaps the most emblematic performance to date was his appearance on the US discussion progrramme *NiteBeat*[11] to discuss his book *The Puppet and the Dwarf*. Immediately apparent to the viewer, there is a sharp visual and auditory disjuncture between the stylish, iridescently dentitioned, smooth-talking TV presenter, Barry Nolan, and the trademark lisping dishevelment of Žižek. Nolan starts by mis-pronouncing Žižek's name, then confesses to finding his book the most difficult thing that he has ever read, and acts in a generally faux-gauche fashion. Underlining the importance of Žižek's emphasis upon the complexly interrelated nature of media form and content, the encounter constitutes two main oppositions: the presenter is urbane and well coiffured, whereas Žižek is effortlessly unkempt and sartorially downbeat; Nolan repeatedly plays up the purported difficulty of Žižek's message, whilst the latter tries equally as hard to explain its fundamental accessibility and everyday applicability.

The following piece of dialogue at least partially conveys how Žižek's presence serves to recalibrate the programme's coordinates so that the presenter's performance inadvertently betrays the normally unrecognized elements of the media SOP:

> *Nolan:* [Introductory comments] Jacques Lacan was a French psychoanalyst. He makes Freud sound like a simple Valley girl. Lacan's theory of how the self works is so complicated it makes my teeth hurt to think about it. [Nolan then clumsily mis-pronounces Žižek's name and home town (Ljubljana). He asks Žižek if he has pronounced his name correctly.]
>
> *Žižek:* [mischievously] I prefer it the wrong way, it makes me paranoiac if I hear it correctly.
>
> *Nolan:* This is the most complicated book that I've ever tried to read.
>
> *Žižek:* Strange because the goal of the book, is on the contrary, is to make Lacan back into someone who even your grandma could understand.

In terms of the discussion's content, Žižek proceeds to demonstrate the claim that his work is accessible by explaining his thesis on postmodern notions of authority. To do this he uses the mundane example of a father requesting his son comes on a Sunday family visit to see his grandmother. In Žižek's interpretation, the traditional father makes the child go to see his grandmother by means of a conventional parental command that brooks no disagreement but is, at least, direct and honest. The nominally super-tolerant, postmodern father, on the other hand, although appearing to be more considerate of his child's feelings, actually persuades his child by means of a type of emotional blackmail. He points out to the child how much it would mean to his grandmother, but more than this, he wheedlingly encourages the child to feel that he should also enjoy the visit. Using this simple situation, Žižek is able to indicate the darker, deeper psychological layers of the everyday. In this particular case, the apparently more enlightened and politically correct father actually represents the more Machiavellian and oppressive of the two parents. The father who assumes the traditional role of the authority figure, in practice, allows his son both to contribute to family bonds and expectations but also retain guilt-free psychological independence as his obedience is obtained at the price of inner resistance and autonomously held recalcitrance. Žižekian makes a similar point about the fake bonhomie that the most ingratiating bosses assume. The boss who makes an effort to be friends with her workers in order to improve the levels of acquiescence to corporate agendas is actually more manipulative than the traditional boss who is open about the direct power relation that she embodies.

The *form* of the exchange between Nolan and Žižek illustrates, in a practical fashion, the *content* of Žižek's essential ideological point. The exchange between the presenter and the guest underscores the distinction to be made between the apparent and actual benignity of the two models of discussant. Although Žižek seems to be a representative of an imposingly traditional, esoteric philosophical domain, the superficially affable TV presenter acts as a closet authoritarian in both what he says and how he says it. Nolan exaggerates the difficulty and underplays the everyday relevance of Žižek's book and thereby seeks to maintain philosophy's place within the 'acceptable' pre-determined bounds of media discourse in which a guest 'plugs' their latest commodified cultural offering without shaking up the socially acceptable coordinates of the interaction. (During the interview, he repeatedly holds up Žižek's book as if to ground the threateningly abstract conversation in a commodity object.) Žižek, meanwhile, although presented as the purveyor of rarefied and foreign esotericism, champions the idea that we should recognize the mundane nature of the oppressive psychological regimes that, on an everyday basis, inhibit our freedom and limit the authenticity of our relationships with others.

More positively, there are times when Žižek's work is welcomed within the media. For example, reviewing for the UK national press *First as Tragedy, Then As Farce*, the literary critic Nicholas Lezard balances Žižek's purportedly occasional impenetrability against the power of his insights. He describes how

[r]eading Žižek is hard work. But it is worth it; like hacking through miles of undergrowth and jungle vegetation in order to be rewarded, every so often, with a splendid view. . . .

I am perhaps not the best person, then, to explicate Žižek, for there are times when I simply do not understand what he is saying. . . . His two intellectual mentors are Hegel and Lacan – and I have also had my problems with them, which is not, of course, to imply that either they or Žižek are charlatans. But one does sometimes yearn for a move away from impenetrability. For when Žižek stops talking like that and actually says something directly, then he is electrifying. It is, I suggest, this tendency, and this one alone, that accounts for his popularity and presence . . . . (Lezard 2009)

Here, despite some enthusiasm for Žižek's project, the media's symbolic violence resides in the call for insights shorn of their philosophical grounding. Even those commentators willing to engage with his message seek to reduce him to the conceptual equivalent of pure caffeine. Instead of the finely balanced entity of both form and content that makes good coffee a rich-tasting, palate-challenging beverage to be savoured, constantly on-the-go, capitalist consumers prefer the intellectual equivalent of the sickly sweet quick hit of the high-energy drink.

THE VIOLENT PHILANTHROPY OF LIBERAL COMMUNISM

Therein resides the true line of separation between radical emancipatory politics and the politics of the status quo: it is not the difference between two different positive visions, sets of axioms, but, rather, the difference between the politics based on a set of universal axioms and the politics which renounces the very constitutive dimension of the political . . . . (*Robespierre*: xxvi)

Žižek's distinction between radical politics and the post-politics of the contemporary mediated status quo was elucidated in Peter Mandelson's own words when, in response to the partial quoting of his alleged statement that 'we [New

Labour] are intensely relaxed about people getting filthy rich', he revealingly made the following correction to the *Guardian* newspaper: 'You quote my comments to California computer executives in 1998 that "we are intensely relaxed about people getting filthy rich" (Leaders, January 11). I do not object to being quoted, as long as I am quoted accurately and in full. What I in fact said on that particular occasion was "as long as they pay their taxes"' (Mandelson 2008). This correction is illuminating for the way in which it underscores Mandelson's genuine values as he refuses to make a political judgement about the *a priori* desirability of a society in which the 'filthy rich' exist. The unethical connotations of 'filthy' are quickly passed over in preference for support of the status quo of an efficient tax regime. The inherent 'fairness' of a democratically constituted tax regime is privileged over the judgement of any inequality that regime generates.

The political value system that Mandelson betrays in this correction partakes of the media-sponsored ideology that Žižek argues is embodied in 'liberal communists [who] give away with one hand what they grabbed with the other' (Žižek 2006a website). Originally seen in such historical figures as Andrew Carnegie, who 'although a man of steel ... had a heart of gold' (ibid.), the liberal communist now appears from the more immaterial world of advanced capitalism in such wealthy individuals as Bill Gates and George Soros. Both the act of consumption and subjects who humanize that process are used by the media to normalize the capitalist paradox, so that

> [t]he structure of the chocolate laxative can be discerned throughout today's ideological landscape; it is what makes a figure like Soros so objectionable. He stands for ruthless financial exploitation combined with its counter-agent, humanitarian worry about the catastrophic social

consequences of the unbridled market economy. Soros's daily routine is a lie embodied: half of his working time is devoted to financial speculation, the other half to 'humanitarian' activities (financing cultural and democratic activities in post-Communist countries, writing essays and books) which work against the effects of his own speculations. (Žižek 2006a website)

Like Mandelson's political calculation, here, the subjective perception of the intrinsic goodness of philanthropic acts of charity outweighs any objective sense of the greater harm caused by the systems from which the philanthropists were able to earn their money in the first place. Both 'filthy rich' tax-payers and liberal communists are absolved from political censure because the tautologically exploitative nature of their laudatory social contribution is ignored. Žižek defines the (anti-)philosophy that informs this non-politics as *post-politics*. Crucially, the political is not repressed but rather foreclosed; it is not considered in the first place. Reflecting the tautological reasoning they are based upon, the efficiency-based judgements of post-politics are highly efficient at avoiding any truly political judgements.

Post-politics embodies in its basic mode of operation key elements of Žižek's overarching approach to ideology. It eliminates politics in the guise of political activity; it is deeply ideological by assuming the appearance of a non-ideological commitment to 'whatever works':

The best formula that expresses the paradox of post-politics is perhaps Tony Blair's characterization of New Labour as the 'Radical Centre' . . . measured by the old standards, the term 'Radical Centre' is the same nonsense as 'radical moderation'. What marked New Labour (or Bill Clinton's politics in the USA) 'radical' is its radical abandonment of

the 'old ideological divides', usually formulated in the guise
of a paraphrase of Deng Xiaoping's motto from the 1960s:
'It doesn't matter if a cat is red or white; what matters is
that it actually catches mice.' . . . It is here that we encounter the gap that separates a political act proper from the
'administration of social matters' which remains within the
framework of existing sociopolitical relations: the political act (intervention) proper is not simply something that
works well within the framework of the existing relations,
but something that *changes the very framework that determines how things work.* To say that good ideas are 'ideas
that work' means that one accepts in advance the (global
capitalist) constellation that determines what works. . . .
One can also put it in terms of the well-known definition
of politics as the 'art of the possible': authentic politics is,
rather, the exact opposite, that is, the art of the *impossible*
– it changes the very parameters of what is considered 'possible' in the existing constellation. (*Ticklish Subject*: 198–9)

The truly dystopian political situation for Žižek is thus not
the Orwellian totalitarian boot stamping upon a human face,
but rather the sterile post-politics of the new administrative
class, highly skilled in media manipulation, whose role is to
remove authentic political questions from social discourse.
The film *Children of Men* (Alfonos Cuarón 2006) evinces this
point. Manifestly portraying an alarming near-future out-
break of mass human infertility, Žižek argues that this theme
merely acts as a cover for the film's latent subject: the existential barrenness of a ruling class with more than a passing
resemblance to today's post-political politicians. Whilst the
social fabric is shown as fraying, the ruling elite are depicted
living in the sterile expanse of a penthouse apartment in
which great works of Western art are exhibited in an asep-
tic, decontextualized fashion. In contrast, poverty-stricken as

it is, the refugee camp in which the apparently last fertile woman alive seeks refuge pulsates with vibrant life. The concept of the liberal communist neatly encapsulates how Žižek's subjective/objective distinction works in practice. Subjectively appearing as good people, these figures are objectively guilty for their role in maintaining the system that causes the very worldwide misery and economic exploitation they so subjectively and publicly donate to alleviate. Žižek cites the historical example of King Leopold II of Belgium, who, although ruling the Congo as a personal fiefdom at the cost of an estimated 10 million deaths, used his exploitation of what was known as the Congo Free State for philanthropic projects back in Belgium. This led him to be known there as the 'Builder King' (*Koning-Bouwer* in Dutch, *le Roi-Bâtisseur* in French). King Leopold's legacy of objective violence continues to this day to the extent that, as pointed out earlier in this chapter but worth repeating, deaths in recent years due to the civil war in the Democratic Republic of the Congo are not known to the *nearest million*. Žižek finds in the Congo perhaps the single biggest example of the power of our mediated society's ability to filter out not only history's but today's gargantuan levels of objective violence in preference for more easily identifiable forms of subjective violence: 'The death of a West Bank Palestinian child, not to mention an Israeli or an American, is mediatically worth thousands of times more than the death of a nameless Congolese' (*Violence*: 2–3)

CONCLUSION: THE DIVINE VIOLENCE OF THE
BRECHTIAN BULLET

Žižek's provocative claim is that, with an appropriate shift of perspective, the adoption of a suitable parallax view, we can see how it is our very attempt to prevent violence that

may actually sustain it. Rather than violence being something the news media disinterestedly transmits as factual
images of violent acts from around the world, violence is
re-conceptualized by Žižek as the innate oppressiveness of
the media's SOP – the powerful and harmful constraints it
imposes upon language and thought despite its purported
neutrality. This is the ideological wheelbarrow which, com-
bining the imagery of Žižek and McLuhan, works to sneak
contraband past the factory security guards of our minds.
For Žižek, the violence we consistently fail to see is that
which is hidden by the apparent normality of the cultural
environments it underlies and depends upon. The rise
in recent decades of celebrity culture provides a forceful
example of the way in which Žižek's seemingly abstract conceptual categories work very practically in social reality. The
manner in which the relatively new[12] celebrity cultural frame
of reference has become the *lingua franca* for the discussion
of a disproportionate number of traditionally political and
economic issues within the media demonstrates a blend of
symbolic and objective violence. Symbolic violence is manifested in the excessive concentration upon celebrity figures
to the exclusion of more politically important issues, and as
this form of symbolic violence becomes the predominant
background value of the media, it enables objective violence
to continue largely unchecked and unquestioned.

Applying Žižek's reasoning to the contemporary mediated
spectacles of Live Eight/Aid, the role of celebrity figures
like Bono and Sir Bob Geldof emphasizes how the media's
subjectively orientated focus is not simply an undesirable,
but essentially harmless, feature of a cultural obsession
with celebrity; rather, it is a role that contributes to enor-
mous international harm. It blocks a clear and unambiguous
acknowledgement of the true cost of objective violence.
Since the media's symbolic violence is systemic, predictably

Žižek himself has not escaped its effects. This is true both in terms of what the media's modes of operation exclude from his discourse (e.g. Lezard's call for decaffeinated, theory-lite versions of Žižek's insights) and the media's subjectivized emphasis upon his eccentric appearance over the content of his thought. A number of press reviewers have preferred to focus upon Žižek's numerous personal quirks and idiosyncrasies rather than deal with the objective implications of his precise argument – a standard reception that ironically illustrates his subjective/objective distinction.[13] Our partial/biased perspective is both an enabling condition and a pervasive ideological outcome of our systemically violent liberal democracies. The media's ideological function can be observed working in a range of situations from Wootton Bassett to the G8 protests. When faced by either peaceful or violent public demonstrations, the media routinely ignores objective critical causes in preference to covering individualized forms of grief and anger. Summarizing Žižek's taxonomy of violence, the media systematically uses symbolic violence to focus upon subjective violence in order to avoid confronting the extent to which our society is based upon a corresponding amount of systemic objective violence.

Žižek's engaged subjective stance thus produces vexed objective questions: he challenges readers to go beyond the politically disengaged subjectivity upon which much of the media is premised (celebrity features, 'human interest'-led news items, etc.) and face up to the radical political implications of what are only nominally neutral processes. Borrowing from Walter Benjamin, Žižek's radical solution to overcome the obfuscation of objective violence draws upon the notion of divine violence defined as the 'brutal intrusions of justice beyond law' (*Violence*: 151). To maximize the counter-intuitive force of his argument, Žižek cites in full Brecht's poem 'The Interrogation of the Good', in which a 'good man' pleads his case in front of a firing squad. Perhaps too blunt for the taste of some readers, the brutality of the sentiment contained within Brecht's verse is designed to highlight the equally horrific nature of the violence we have become accustomed to ignoring *as a matter of course*. The 'good man' uses the defence of good intentions, to which Brecht responds in kind, so that, in contrast to the moral evasiveness and political casuistry that accompanies the media's symbolic violence, the final lines of Brecht's poem unambiguously present the form of violence necessary to countervail the objective violence we frequently struggle to see as anything other than the unfortunate consequence of deeply 'good' intentions:

> We shall put you in front of a good wall and shoot you
> With a good bullet from a good gun and bury you
> With a good shovel in the good earth.
>
> (Bertolt Brecht[14])

Differing degrees of willingness to confront the objective consequences of subjectively framed acts is what distinguishes the 'sophisticated primitive' from the 'naïve cynic' – or, in terms that we shall now explore, the ideologically serious Joker from the noble liar.

6

THE JOKER'S LITTLE SHOP OF IDEOLOGICAL HORRORS

INTRODUCTION: THE DEADLY JESTER

... there may come a time when we find that being a psychoanalyst means having a place in society. That place will, I hope, I am sure, be taken, even if it is for the moment occupied only by psychoanalysts who have lurched into their little joke shop. (Lacan 2008: 49)

Amongst his critics, Žižek is viewed as both a jester and a dangerous thinker[1] (and sometimes both – simultaneously – as in the description 'The Deadly Jester'[2]). The jester slur requires either the deliberate or unwitting failure to appreciate the paradoxical seriousness of Žižek's frequent recourse to jokes as explored throughout the previous chapters, whilst the perception that he is dangerous betrays an anxious recognition that his theoretical insights have the power to disturb conventional understandings of media content. As Lacan argues above, today the psychoanalyst is a relatively marginalized figure within society, condemned for the time being to 'their little joke shop'. In Žižek's role as a psychoanalyst of culture, the relative marginality of his position (his media presence is big only in comparison to the standard academic profile) is maintained by the media's portrayal of his serious political argument as facetious postmodern relativism. This previously encountered charge is explored in more detail in this chapter in relation to the traumatic events of 9/11 to demonstrate more clearly still the distinctly non-relativist core of Žižek's radical media critique highlighted throughout this book. The sober radical reasons for his constant recourse to jokes and obscene examples is then further examined through the darkly evocative movie character of the Joker.

Whilst he is not averse to using examples taken from art-house cinema (e.g. in this chapter the notion of trauma is examined in the light of Michael Haneke's *The Piano Teacher*), the ideological issues Žižek wants to highlight are most prevalent and active in his preferred *metier*: the analyis of Hollywood films. As an illustration, the chapter refers in detail to the Batman films directed by Tim Burton and Christopher Nolan. Containing a range of deceptively grotesque characters like the Penguin and the Joker and addressing dark social themes via a stylish neo-Gothic aesthetic, Burton and Nolan's films provide a particularly useful analytical resource with which to develop in more depth the argument delineated in earlier chapters: that today, liberal democracy frequently achieves its most powerful ideological effects through the appearance of being non-ideological. The oversized and manic animal characters contained within the Batman films are much more ideologically significant than their apparent status as comic characters might suggest. A more nuanced understanding of their wider cultural roles helps us to gain valuable insight into the politically charged relationship that exists between fantasy and politics, whether experienced in such exceptionally traumatic events as 9/11, or the dark escapist comfort of a multiplex cinema. In this chapter it is argued that the true jokers are those who fail to recognize the society-defining reality of this relationship.

WELCOME TO THE JUST DESERTS OF THE REAL: 9/11 AND FUNDAMENTALIST REACTIONS TO THEORY

'America got what it fantasised about' – which Žižek insinuates, echoing Baudrillard, is merely another way of saying *that America got what it had coming.* . . . Amid the fog of postmodern relativism disseminated by Baudrillard, Žižek, and others, something essential is missing. (Wolin 2004: 307)

Žižek is a fashionable Slovenian 'cultural theorist' and author of books on Jacques Lacan, Lenin and David Lynch . . . but he is perhaps most famous for his judgement on 9/11: 'In a way, America got what it fantasised about.'
     That 'in a way' is pure Žižek: moral relativism masked by rhetorical evasion. (Bearn 2004)

Wolin and Bearn's above criticisms of Žižek provide strong illustrations of psychological projection. Thus, in the very instance of accusing Žižek of insinuation, Wolin commits that same act by conflating Žižek's consideration of fantasy as a well-established psychological phenomenon with an unfounded accusation that Žižek thought America received its just deserts. Both writers project on to Žižek the charge of relativism – one that is curious considering the consistently qualmless and direct manner with which Žižek argues throughout his work for the better identification of the

sources of power, and his insistence upon attributing responsibility for the consequences of power to those who exercise
it. A repressed antipathy to theory is betrayed by Bearn for
putting 'cultural theorist' in quotation marks, implying as
it does that theorizing about culture is somehow a dubious
activity. Taken together, Wolin and Bearn's dual misap-
prehension stems from their failure to understand that, far
from being fuelled by relativism, Žižek's analysis of fantasy
demonstrates how it plays a powerful structuring role in our
real, pragmatic lives – life without fantasies is *essentially* not
possible. Žižek's precise point about the media's coverage of
9/11 was that, irrespective of any feelings of just desert based
upon a vindictive sense of *schadenfreude*, the 9/11 tragedy was
so traumatic precisely because the images of that day had
already appeared in a spate of Hollywood movies. Žižek's
'morally relativistic' theoretical point was empirically demonstrated by Hollywood executives' decision immediately
after 9/11 to postpone such films as *Big Trouble*, *Collateral
Damage*, *Sidewalks of New York*, and *The Last Castle* for exactly
that reason.

In direct opposition to the claim that Žižek's approach is
characterized by 'moral relativism masked by rhetorical eva-
sion', his umambiguously direct position has been clear from
the beginning of his first internationally recognized book.
Thus, Part 1 of *The Sublime Object of Ideology* (1989) encapsulates the political philosophy of the mass media that Žižek
develops to confront the ideological role played by the intangible but immensely powerful psychological phenomena of
fantasy and belief. Žižek blends Marx's notion of commodity
fetishism with Lacan's psychoanalytical categories in order
to show more powerfully than is possible with conventional
social science analysis alone the profoundly important role
played in ideological discourse by belief, irrational attachment, and the subtle effects experienced due to the way in

which rational decision-making may be overridden by excessive familiarity with ideological processes and effects.

> The contemporary hegemonic ideological scene is thus split between . . . two modes of fetishism, the cynical and the fundamentalist, both impervious to 'rational argumentative' criticism. While the fundamentalist ignores (or at least mistrusts) argumentation, blindly clinging to his fetish, the cynic pretends to accept argumentation, but ignores its symbolic efficiency. In other words, while the fundamentalist (not so much believes as) directly 'knows' the truth embodied in his fetish, the cynic practises the logic of disavowal ('I know very well, but . . .'). (*Tragedy*: 68–9)

The cynic's suspension of belief in the ultimate primacy of rational argument evolves into a working belief in cynicism itself. Thus, no matter how badly Really Existing Capitalism fails, and is proved to fail as much as Really Existing Socialism ever did, the cynic stubbornly persists in a more 'realistic' set of beliefs/clichés like the notion that because 'people are basically selfish, there are no other alternatives to capitalism'. The fundamentalist, by contrast, is not even willing to countenance this less-than-ideal, pragmatic accommodation. He or she knows directly that capitalism works, and any evidence to the contrary is merely proof that it is not being left alone sufficiently to achieve its inherent potential. Thus, at the time of a deep recession, Ayn Rand continues to sell 800,000 books a year in the US (see Hari 2009).

Post 9/11, Western contemporary TV news discourse was unsurprisingly dominated by the issue of Islamic fundamentalism rather than its own forms of fundamentalist capitalist belief. In the media's SOP, the fundamentalist Other embodies an essentially different set of ideals to that which binds the rest of us – one-dimensional fanatics are needed to create, by means of contrast, a more tangible sense of meaning that capitalism otherwise lacks. Žižek argues that really authentic fundamentalists, whether they be Tibetan Buddhists or the Amish, are marked by 'the absence of resentment and envy, the deep indifference towards the non-believers' way of life' (*Violence*: 72). Instead of irresolvable cultural differences with the West, the real problem with groups like Al-Qaeda is 'the opposite fact that the fundamentalists are already like us, that secretly, they have already internalized our standards and measure themselves by them. . . . Paradoxically, what the fundamentalists really lack is precisely a dose of that true "racist" conviction of one's own superiority' (ibid.: 73). For Žižek, rather than constituting an externally derived threat to capitalism, the roots of Islamic fundamentalism stem from an attempt to fill the void created by capitalism's own inherent lack of meaning. From this perspective, Islamic fundamentalism is a historical reaction to, and adaptation of, capitalism's own symbolic violence – the manner in which capitalism expunges all that is particular in the service of a universal drive, a drive without any ultimate content beyond its own tautological need for endless circulation and further expansion. Al-Qaeda's adaptation of this mode of circulation as an end in itself became the endlessly repeated media spectacle of the 9/11 images of destruction.

Both the strategy behind the 9/11 attacks and the media's subsequent constant repetition of the images of the Twin Towers' collapse (but signal failure to understand its essential geo-political significance) constituted, from radically different political orientations, a dramatic visual representation of capitalism's truth-without-meaning. Rather than being a totally alien organizational form, Al-Qaeda directly (if perversely) mirrors the Western economic model of the franchise operation. Similarly, as noted in the previous chapter, when the military response to 9/11 transmuted into confrontation with Iraq, Comical Ali's performances in front of the cameras presciently reflected what proved to be the grossly inaccurate claims of success made by the Western media's own talking heads. Both the terrorists, deprived of their own self-sufficient ideology owing to the internalization of Western values, and an America lacking a comparable strength of belief have been reduced to the acting out that takes place as an ideological displacement for want of effective alternatives. However, amidst the similarities, and although creating a spectacle tailored for Western media consumption, there was an element of the 9/11 fundamentalism that jarred with capitalist logic. The hijackers were exchanging their lives for a belief unto death in a manner that could not be met by a society whose President requested in response that people go to Disney World in Florida (Bacevich 2008) and whose military reaction was to declare war upon an abstract noun – the inchoate *War on Terror*.

To illustrate the basic psychological processes at work in traumatic situations such as 9/11, Žižek usefully (and much to the ire of conservative critics) draws upon Michael Haneke's *The Piano Teacher* (2002), based upon Elfriede Jelink's novel of the same name. The film's protagonist is like the fundamentalist 'who becomes the *dupe of his fantasy* . . . [she] lacks the coordinates of the fantasy which would allow her to organize her desire' (*Parallax*: 354). The piano teacher engages in a torrid relationship with a young male pupil and, following a perversely step-by-step detailed description of her sexual fantasies delineated in a letter, she is raped when the student acts out the letter's content. Žižek's understanding of the fantasy's function privileges rather than relativizes its truly traumatic nature. Most incisively of all, he adds a crucial further speculation: '. . . what if the fantasy she puts in the letter she gives her lover is *his own* fantasy of what he would really like to do to her, so that he is disgusted precisely because he gets from her directly his own fantasy?' (ibid.: 355). It is this additional insight that illuminates a crucial blind spot within the Western media. We are very familiar with the notion that the fundamentalist is duped by his own fantasy – in our eyes, his belief, like the piano teacher's, is too explicit and excessively literal. However, we find it much more difficult to recognize the extent to which Lacan's counter-intuitive claim that *les non-dupes errent* (the non-duped err) is applicable to our own condition. Like the shock experienced by the piano teacher's student at seeing his own fantasy reflected back to him, 9/11 traumatized a nation precisely because it saw its own Hollywood-like fantasies of destruction suddenly materialized in an all-too-real event.

In his specific psychoanalytical use of the term 'fantasy', Žižek clearly and explicitly argues the *opposite* position to that claimed by Wolin and Bearn:

> ... while (some) women effectively may daydream about being raped, this fact not only in no way legitimizes the actual rape – it makes it even more violent. Let us take two women, the first, liberated and assertive, active; the other, secretly daydreaming about being brutally handled by her partner, even raped. The crucial point is that, if both of them are raped, the rape will be much more traumatic for the second one, on account of the very fact that it will realize in 'external' social reality the 'stuff of her dreams'. (Žižek 2007b)

In a case of rape, prior fantasy reinforces and exacerbates any later experience in reality that resonates with that fantasy; it has nothing whatsoever to do with questions of desert or moral relativism. In psychoanalytical treatment, there is a therapeutic need to 'traverse the fantasy': that is, to confront and take responsibility for the fundamental (essentializing) fantasies that structure our lives. Because Žižek, like any good analyst, raises issues that are inevitably traumatic for the patient/reader, excessively emotional reactions projected back on to Žižek are perhaps to be expected. In their unwillingness to engage with the basic, practical significance of fantasy for the broader social environment, Wolin and Bearn unwittingly demonstrate the usefulness of other psychoanalytical concepts: denial and negative transference.

Žižek's mode of *looking awry* and adopting a *parallax view* takes seriously the powerful structuring role of fantasy. It is particularly suited to interrogate what the earlier chapters have shown to be the knotty imbrication of belief, disavowal, and unconscious acceptance that characterizes our contemporary society of the spectacle. The media coverage of 9/11 and the subsequent *War on Terror* encapsulate key aspects of the nature of belief in a heavily mediated cultural environment. The political consequences of this clash between the West's form of mediated belief and Islamic fundamentalism (which the West did much to create) are explored in pieces both Baudrillard and Žižek wrote soon after the 9/11 tragedy: *The Spirit of Terrorism* (2002) and *Welcome to the Desert of the Real* (2002), respectively. Baudrillard distinguishes between a notion of *symbolic exchange* motivating the plane hijackers that contrasted with the capitalist order of *signs* that enframed the US response. He interprets the hijackers' actions as demonstrating a form of belief held much more directly and viscerally than tends to be possible within the society they targeted. For Žižek, to return to Chapter 4's treatment of contemporary cynical belief, Western media forms tend to produce their effects whilst appearing not to, so that the viewer can say, ' "I pretend to pretend to believe" which means: "I really believe without being aware of it"' (*Parallax*: 354).

The archetypal example of this kind of ideological

operation are the notions of commodity fetishism and electronic/paper money. We pretend to believe that money made of paper/bytes is actually worth the physical goods we buy with it and that commodities have special properties (we pay extra for the sign value of the Nike swoosh) whilst simultaneously claiming that we don't *really* believe. Žižek's key point is that conscious disavowal contradictorily co-exists with practical acts that embody belief. By contrast: 'In the case of the so-called "fundamentalists," this "normal functioning" of ideology in which the ideological belief is transposed onto the Other is disturbed by the violent return of the immediate belief – they "really believe it"' (ibid.: 354). Žižek slices through this Gordian knot of ideology created between these two fundamentally different value systems caught in a communicational deadlock. He demonstrates the process by which capitalist beliefs were sublimated into fictional representations that phantasmatically prefigured the trauma of the real-world events created by the clash of Western culture (*pace* Huntington 1996) with those who *really do believe*. Thus in the Wachowski brothers' *The Matrix* (1999):

> . . . when the hero (played by Keanu Reeves) awakens into the 'real reality,' he sees a desolate landscape littered with burned ruins – what remained of Chicago after a global war. The resistance leader Morpheus utters the ironic greeting: 'Welcome to the desert of the real.' Was it not something of the similar order that took place in New York on September 11? Its citizens were introduced to the 'desert of the real' – to us, corrupted by Hollywood, the landscape and the shots we saw of the collapsing towers could not but remind us of the most breathtaking scenes in the catastrophe big productions. When we hear how the bombings were a totally unexpected shock, how the unimaginable *Impossible* happened, one should recall the other defining

catastrophe from the beginning of the 21st century, that of *Titanic*: it was also a shock, but the space for it was already prepared in ideological fantasizing, since *Titanic* was the symbol of the might of the 19th century industrial civilization.[3] Does the same not hold also for these bombings? Not only were the media bombarding us all the time with the talk about the terrorist threat; this threat was also obviously libidinally invested – just recall the series of movies from *Escape From New York* to *Independence Day*. The unthinkable which happened was thus the object of fantasy: in a way, **America got what it fantasized about**, and this was the greatest surprise. (Žižek 2001 website [emboldening added])

Contra Wolin and Bearn, for Žižek, an undeniably important, deeply non-relativist, element of 9/11's emotional impact was the traumatic sense that we had already seen it before – *in our fantasies*. This is what Freud meant when he said 'an uncanny effect often arises when the boundary between fantasy and reality is blurred, when we are faced with the reality of something that we have until now considered imaginary, when a symbol takes on the full function and significance of what it symbolizes'. (Freud 2003 [1899–1919]: 150). It was the way in which this directly felt sense of unreality so invasively entered our day-to-day reality that made 9/11 such a particularly distressing spectacle.

THE COMMUNIST JOKER: THE METHOD IN ŽIŽEK'S MADNESS

Shakespeare gives an essential role in his plays to those characters that are called fools, court jesters whose position allows them to uncover the most hidden motives, the character traits that cannot be discussed frankly without violating the norms of proper conduct. It's not a matter of mere impudence and insults. What they say proceeds basically by way of ambiguity . . . we must not neglect the *way* in which Hamlet feigns madness, his way of plucking ideas out of the air, opportunities for punning equivocation, to dazzle his enemies with the brilliance of an inspired moment – all of which give his speech an almost maniacal quality. . . . Everything that Hamlet says, and at the same time the reactions of those around him, constitute as many problems in which the audience is constantly losing its bearings. (Lacan et al. 1977: 33–4)

At first glance, the highly popular Batman films (specifically Tim Burton's *Batman* [1989], *Batman Returns* [1992], and Christopher Nolan's *Batman Begins* [2005], *The Dark Knight* [2008]) are superficial, fantastical movies based upon escapist comic books and distant from 'serious' socio-political issues. A Žižekian reading, however, demonstrates the way in which they act as particularly good examples of sublime objects of ideology – embodiments of capitalist ideology in the very guise of non-ideological ephemera. In the following excerpt from *The Dark Knight*, speaking to the District Attorney, Harvey Dent, a representative figure of the law, the Joker explains how:

[n]obody panics when they expect people to get killed. Nobody panics when things go according to plan, even if the plans are horrifying. If I tell the press that tomorrow a gangbanger will get shot, or a truckload of soldiers will get blown up, nobody panics. But when I say one little old mayor will die, everyone loses their minds! Introduce a little anarchy, you upset the established order, and everything becomes chaos. I am an agent of chaos. And you know the thing about chaos, Harvey? It's fair.

The Joker's justification of chaos vividly illustrates: Žižek's distinction between subjective and objective violence; Lacan's previous interpretation of the disorientation created in the audience of *Hamlet*; as well as Fredric Jameson's (1992) notion of *cognitive mapping* – a phrase he uses to convey a sense of the need to develop conceptual aids with which to orientate ourselves within the discombobulating fluxes and flows of postmodern consumer society. Additionally, the Joker's words resonate closely with Lacan's above interpretation of Hamlet's disruptive presence and Žižek's observation that '[t]he problem is today that when you have chaos and disorder people lose their cognitive mapping' (Žižek interview, Thornhill 2009). In relation to Žižek's Diogenes-like provocations, the psychologically perturbing but politically insightful role played by the character of the Joker (and the other Batman films' assorted half-comic, half-villainous figures) throws up some interesting parallels.

Pejoratively labelled a jester, Žižek shares the Joker's interest in chaos. However, whilst the Joker is a self-described agent of chaos feeding upon society's disorientation, Žižek is devoted to the search for cognitive mapping. Like Žižek, the Joker is a fascinatingly entertaining character, but the strength of their performances threatens to distract us from the radical political implications of their core message. This is a recognizable trait of the media's coverage of charismatic individuals. Henry Louis Taylor observed that we suffer from collective amnesia over the actual political content of Martin Luther King's dream: 'Everyone knows, even the smallest kid knows about Martin Luther King, can say his most famous moment was that "I have a dream" speech. No one can go further than that one sentence. All we know is that this guy had a dream. We don't know what that dream was' (cited in *Tragedy*: 37–8). Dr King's politics exceeded race: he campaigned on anti-war and poverty issues and was in Memphis at the time of his death in order to support striking sanitation workers. It is this substantive political content that has largely been lost in the more iconic, but limited, image we now have of Dr King as only a civil rights leader. Similarly, *The Dark Knight* is widely recognized as a disturbing film, particularly the performance of the soon-to-die Heath Ledger, but very few people are able to articulate precisely, beyond its obviously dark Gothic aesthetic, why the film resonates so deeply with its audience.

Žižek questions whether the film's impact stems from the fact it 'touches a nerve of our ideologico-political constellation: the undesirability of truth' (Žižek 2009b). In both Jack Nicholson and Heath Ledger's portrayals, the Joker touches a nerve both verbally – he constantly and entertainingly provides cutting, on-going critiques of officialdom's cant – and also in terms of the deliberately spectacular-based nature of his actions that undermine officialdom's version of the truth. In one particularly revealing episode in *The Dark Knight*, the Joker gatecrashes a Bruce Wayne soirée and ostentatiously throws from his glass the champagne that Wayne had been discarding surreptitiously – an incident representative of their contrasting attitudes to the relationship between appearance and reality. But perhaps the single most memorable example of the Joker's iconoclasm is provided in *Batman* by Jack Nicholson's Debordian *dérive* at the Gotham City Art Museum. To the accompaniment of music by the-artist-formally-known-as-Prince, the Joker and his accomplices cavort whilst defacing and smashing paintings and sculptures (although the Joker stops at Francis Bacon's *Figure with Meat* to observe, 'I kinda like this one, Bob, leave it'). Whilst the Joker's maniacally unkempt appearance and destructive acts are a source of obvious shock and disturbance, what arguably touches the contemporary nerve most is, as with Žižek himself, the extent to which, beneath the surface-level oddness of their performances, there lies an unnervingly unadorned truth. Whereas the Joker and Žižek wear their oddness openly, nearly all the other key Gotham City characters wear masks, literally in the case of Batman, or by presenting different faces to different constituencies. This is a tendency that culminates in *The Dark Knight* when the District Attorney Harvey Dent becomes two-faced as half of his face is horribly disfigured.

Žižek asks, 'Who, then, is Joker who wants to disclose the truth beneath the Mask, convinced that this disclosure will destroy the social order? He is not a man without mask, but, on the contrary, a man fully identified with his mask, a man who IS his mask – there is nothing, no "ordinary guy," beneath his mask' (Žižek 2009b website). In further answer to Žižek's rhetorical question, the Joker acts as a running commentary upon social hypocrisy, obviously in the form of the scathing things he says, but also by the way in which the carelessness of his outward appearance contrasts sharply with those who surround him, whether they be the social elite of Gotham (the Joker's entrances are all the more dramatic for the manner in which they represent an intrusion of the unaffected into image-conscious high-society gatherings), or Batman's precisely engineered costumes and hi-tech bat-couture accoutrements. An additional element of the Joker's puncturing of social niceties is the way in which, even when he tells lies, he does so in the service of a deeper truth. He resolutely refuses to engage in the therapeutic language others might use to explain how his actions have been determined by his facial disfigurement: 'This is why Joker has no back-story and lacks any clear motivation: he tells different people different stories about his scars, mocking the idea that he should have some deep-rooted trauma that drives him' (ibid.). At least part of the Joker's unsettling impact is due to the way he disrupts the postmodern mode of cognitive mapping by which we self-deludedly accommodate ourselves to the systemic distortions of life under capitalism.

The Joker incisively highlights the precise nature of our libidinal investments in the status quo, raising uncomfortable truths in the process. His rationale is his lack of rationale. He deliberately embodies the senselessness of a capitalist social system in which death and destruction are tolerated as long as they can feasibly be understood as part of a plan. In stark contrast, he is determined to make people question the fundamental justification of this plan. This is what lies behind his repeated refusal to explain his own behaviour through a consistent story – by telling various versions of how he became disfigured. His explanation is that there is no ultimate easy explanation. The Joker represents an honest counterpart to the contemporary tendency to resort to therapy-speak to excuse our actions. Here Žižek cites the behaviour of the hypothetical neo-Nazi skinhead who is emblematic of postmodern cynicism because, when necessary, he resorts to excusing his unacceptably racist behaviour as the result of childhood trauma. Unlike the skinhead, the Joker, daubed in face paint to exaggerate his disfigurement, literally *faces up* to society's traumatic core: our constitutive dependence upon levels of violence we would prefer to disavow.

GOTHAM CITY VILLAINS AS CAPITALISM'S BAD CONSCIENCE: 'WHAT YOU PLACE IN YOUR TOILET, I PLACE ON MY MANTLE'

> . . . – he's an ascetic without a real history. Rather, his only goal and source of pleasure is in making his victims face up to the abstracted violent substructure around which their culture is configured. . . . [T]he Joker provides a scarred face to the invisible logic of capitalism, with cracking make-up

and a forced smile. He's pure desire without an object, paradoxically making the impersonal personal and invisible visible. ... The Joker is the same unbounded desire that drives capitalism. Without any object or goal to satisfy him, he exists outside of our rational system and can only be stopped with violence. He can't be beat, however, only beaten, because the solution to the problem he presents is the problem itself: repression of systemic violence. (Reece 2008)

It is because of his unique embodiment of both what he says *and* what he does (unlike the Bruce Wayne/Batman dichotomy and the literal and metaphorical two-faced nature of the pre- and post-accident Harvey Dent) that the Joker is such a powerfully affecting figure. Taken together, his larger-than-life appearance, laughter, and actions all reflect the normally repressed and invisible elements of the capitalist system. The unashamed asceticism that Adorno attributed to high art is incorporated by the Joker in relation to the purity of his drive, but the sophisticated form of his various stunts also offers a satirical aesthetic critique of low culture's corollary: the pornographic violence and spectacle-dependent nature of contemporary life. This occurs in two main forms:

1 The Joker self-consciously makes use of the Gotham press and TV to make his points, and he typically enters public spaces with a mind to creating spectacular events.
2 The Joker acts as a dark mirror-image of both the society and its superhero representative that he seeks to undermine.

The latter of these two elements provides *The Dark Knight* with an ideological richness of theme that illustrates well the instructive appropriateness of Žižek's high theory/low culture mix. The Joker raises disheartening questions about the real nature of society's need for a heroic crime-fighting fantasy figure – a symbol upon which its fantasies can be projected (once again, literally, considering the Bat-Signal used to call Batman to its rescue). The extent to which we are disturbed by the Joker is directly related to the manner in which he makes visible what is normally repressed in society. By acting so directly as a thematic counterpoint to Batman, as described by Reece above, the Joker enables a face (distorted as it is) to be put upon the irrational aspect of capitalism that we know at one level to exist, but at another level we refuse to accept. The ideological role of the Joker is in fact a deeply serious one.

An ambiguous tone of the Batman series of films resides in the intertwining of similarities and differences between the eponymous hero and his various nemeses. An unusual feature of this particular superhero is the explicit way in which his character contains dark elements of symbolism that might normally be expected to be seen in the portrayal of villains. Paradoxically, whilst Batman is presented as a hopeful figure appearing from the shadows of the night, the menace of the criminal characters comes from their clownish appearance. The Joker is a clear example of the menacing effect achieved through over-identification with otherwise non-threatening imagery, but so too is the Penguin, a conventionally humorous animal who, in *Batman Returns*, although travelling in a ludicrously oversized yellow duck-boat, also provides a disconcerting embodiment of the obscene underside of power. For example, in a Clintonesque parody of political discourse, he learns from the capitalist Max Shreck who bank-rolls him how to perform and speak in a clichéd manner to suit the cameras: 'I may have saved the Mayor's baby but I refuse to save a Mayor who stood by helpless as a baby.' Closely juxtaposed to such glib rhetoric are crude misogynistically laced comments. When a female admirer at a photo-opportunity set up by Shreck says, 'You're the coolest role-model a young person could have,' the Penguin retorts: 'And you're the hottest young person a role model could have.' After lasciviously placing a campaign badge on her chest, he again parodically reflects: 'The Mayor stuff is not about power. It's about reaching out to people, touching people, groping people.' Finally, he meets Catwoman with the comment, 'Just the pussy I've been waiting for.'

This acting out of the sexually obscene underside of power has already been prefigured by the Penguin's earlier uncovering of politics' obscene underside. When Shreck first meets the Penguin, he is subjected to a damning critique of his own immorality whilst the Penguin spins a spiral-patterned umbrella – a visual allusion to the self-hypnosis we put ourselves under in order not to see the root truth of our social situation. The Penguin observes that: 'Odd as it may seem, Max, you and I have something in common: We're both perceived as monsters. But somehow, you're a respected monster and I am, to date, not!' Shreck defends himself: 'Frankly, I feel that's a bum rap. I'm a businessman. Tough, yes, shrewd, okay, but that does not make me a monster.' To which the Penguin retorts: 'Don't embarrass yourself, Max. I know all about you. What you hide, I discover. What you place in your toilet, I place on my mantle. Get the picture?' This final phrase, along with the Jack Nicholson Joker's statement that 'This town needs an enema', could be taken as epigraphs for Žižek's theoretical illumination of mass culture. Like Žižek, the villains in Batman films are united by their desire to peel back appearances to discover the truth beneath. The Penguin wants 'recognition of my basic humanity. But most of all, I want to find out who I am.' Like the Joker, and Catwoman ('Who's the man behind the bat? Maybe you can help me find the woman behind the cat?'), the Penguin is on a genuine voyage of self-discovery, whereas the 'good' characters from the legal and political establishment in the Batman films tend, as at the end of *The Dark Knight*, to defend the social necessity of the noble lies that prevent society reflecting too long or closely upon its foundational assumptions.

The Penguin seeks to pull back the mask of Shreck's commercial two-facedness (Penguin: 'Remember, Max, you flush it, I flaunt it'), just as the Joker seeks to uncover Batman's mask and the ghoulishly traumatic unveiling of Harvey Dent's hypocrisy through his literal two-faced deformity. Even the relatively minor character of Catwoman uncovers repression – in the form of sexuality. She transforms from a dowdy secretary to a male-fantasy rubber-suit-wearing sex-kitten. In the process, she makes a series of sexually charged comments, ranging from her early allusions of frustration contained within her conversations with her cat: 'Back from more sexual escapades you refuse to share? Not that I'd pry' to the subsequent explicit quip: 'You poor guys – always confusing your pistols with your privates.' Despite these elements of the Batman films that reveal surface-level hypocrisy, the overall ideological effect of their portrayal of Gotham City society is one of containment and the obfuscation of any genuinely radical interpretation of capitalism. This effect is achieved from the way in which the films act in Žižek's terms as forms of constituent rather than constituted ideology.

BATMAN AS CONSTITUENT IDEOLOGY: THE LIBERAL COMMUNIST

... one should distinguish between constituted ideology
– empirical manipulations and distortions at the level of
content – and constituent ideology – the ideological form
which provides the coordinates of the very space within

which the content is located. ... Today, this fundamental
level of constituent ideology assumes the guise of its very
opposite, of non-ideology. (Žižek 2009b website)

The notion of constituent ideology is encapsulated in the
stolen wheelbarrow anecdote. We lose focus upon the ideological effects of form by over-concentrating upon nominal
content, and a vivid illustration of this process is provided by
the Batman films. At the level of constituted ideology, the
films contain a quite radical critique of advanced capitalism
– Gotham City is a dark (literally in terms of the cinema-
tography) dystopian place in which private affluence exists
cheek-by-jowl with public squalor. However, the form in
which the films are structured, and the manner in which
their potentially radical messages are processed, produce
a different, non-constituted, overall ideological effect: the
constituent processing of potential critique by means of various caricatures and symbols. *The Dark Knight*, for example,
not only deals explicitly with the issue of the basic corrup-
tion of individual public figures, but it also strongly portrays
the deep-rooted cynicism of the whole political and economic ruling class. It thereby clearly demonstrates a working
awareness of the form that constituent ideology assumes.
However, instead of then exploring a radical solution to this
ideological problem, it merely provides a more sophisticated
further form of constituent ideology (the film form itself)
with which to befog possible solutions. The movie exempli-
fies 'the contemporary cynical attitude: in it, ideology can lay
its cards on the table, reveal the secret of its functioning, and
still continue to function' (*Indivisible Remainder*: 200; 1997b
website) – the ideology of the stolen wheelbarrow.

The ideologically constituent aspect of the films is most
clearly embodied in the figure of the liberal communist,
Bruce Wayne: 'Capitalism needs charity in the same way the

Batman "justifies" Bruce Wayne's wealth. Capitalism qua Gotham City creates the problems and then provides the repressive mask by which those problems are to be solved' (Reece 2008). The systemic problems with capitalism are represented in the films as the failings of individual capitalists like Max Shreck and their underworld counterparts such as the Joker and the Penguin who take things to unacceptable extremes. The implicit message of the movies is that the philanthropic capitalist model enshrined in the Wayne family legacy is the solution to society's problems, and this is what Batman fights to protect – *le nom du père* – his father's benign legacy. The films thereby subjectivize objective, systemic problems and provide a sustained example of the conceptual distinction Žižek makes between subjective and objective forms of violence. The films achieve this effect through the constituently conservative form in which they present their constituted ideological content – an only apparently radical portrayal of capitalism's dark soul. Batman's origins may lie within the comic book, but the Hollywood movies embody a serious political issue: the specific nature of contemporary mediated belief.

We have seen in Chapter 4's distinction between 'primitive' and postmodern belief how today's belief relies upon an unacknowledged distance between belief and action – we pretend that we pretend to believe. The result is that, despite our surface-level cynicism, our continual acting as if we did believe creates its own symbolic efficiency and we do in fact come to believe notwithstanding our own protestations to the contrary:

> At the level of belief, key capitalist ideas – commodities are animate; capital has a quasi-natural status – are repudiated but it is precisely the ironic distance from such notions that allows us to *act* as if they are true. The disavowal of the

beliefs allows us to perform the actions. Ideology, then, depends upon the conviction that what 'really matters' is what we are, rather than what we do, and that 'what we are' is defined by an 'inner essence'. (Fisher 2006)

Whereas the distance held towards his belief by the primitive is a conscious one, our disbelief is mediated by key capitalist mechanisms – the marketplace, the media – so that Kant's subjectively objective (a reality interpreted by the subject) becomes the objectively subjective (the subject interpreted/ interpellated by reality). 'Although people may claim not to believe in the political system, their inert cynicism only validates that system . . . the idea that the way we behave in society is determined by objective market forces rather than subjective beliefs' (Thornhill 2009). This introduces a significant degree of ambiguity to Rachel Dawes' words at the end of *Batman Begins*: 'Bruce . . . deep down you may still be that same great kid you used to be. But it's not who you are underneath . . . it's what you do that defines you.'

A crucial difference between Žižek and both the Joker and Batman is that Žižek maintains the necessary conscious distance between his acts and his beliefs, whereas the Joker takes Rachel's words further than she could envisage by maniacally removing the distance completely so that he actually becomes his mask. Meanwhile, Batman cynically hides behind his mask. He thinks of it as a mere symbol but thereby fails to recognize its profound symbolic efficiency and the impact it has upon his own psyche. Whereas the Joker disowns any founding principles (giving a different explanation of his facial disfigurement each time), Žižek remains loyally consistent to his key theoretical influences. Whilst the Joker commits himself to chaos for its own sake, Žižek has a clear rational motivation: to make society traverse its fundamental fantasy. What Žižek's critics either can't, or don't want to, see is the manner in which (like Batman but unlike the Joker) Žižek is conscious of the necessity of masks, but also (like the Joker and unlike Batman) the need to take responsibility for these masks.

The Batman series' Gothic (Gotham) fantasy represents a form of recuperated trauma with which to avoid confronting the much more Gothic reality of really existing capitalism. In *Batman Begins*, frank recognition of the problem with capitalism is avoided by means of both constituted and constituent ideology. Capitalism's faults are portrayed as a result of its individual failures, not its innate structure – the Wayne family are philanthropic; they built a monorail for the people. Revealingly, however, by the end of the film this relationship breaks down, as symbolized by the destruction of the monorail to avoid the phantasmatic rising of the proletarian masses caused by the Scarecrow's weaponized hallucinogenic (reminiscent of Marx's 'there is a spectre haunting Europe'), reinforced by R'as Al Ghul's League of Shadows (read Communist League). Buttressing the process by which disbelief acted upon cynically becomes its own form of belief, the symbolic efficiency of various masks and costumes is presented cynically. There are frequent verbal and visual references within the Batman films to the ludicrous nature of the various characters' costumes. (Bruce Wayne, in particular, makes various self-deprecatory comments about his bat costume, but nevertheless, Batman still represents 'the hero Gotham deserves'.) An attitude of superficial cynicism to symbols that runs throughout the films clouds the deep seriousness of the ideological role played by those same symbols.

CONCLUSION: THE NOBLE LIE

This necessity of a lie to sustain public morale is *The Dark Knight*'s final message: only a lie can redeem us. No wonder that, paradoxically, the only figure of truth in the film is Joker, its supreme villain. The goal of his terrorist attacks on Gotham City is made clear: they will stop when Batman will take off his mask and reveal his true identity; to prevent this disclosure and thus protect Batman, Dent tells the press that he is Batman – another lie. In order to entrap Joker, Gordon stages his own (fake) death – yet another lie . . . (Žižek 2009b website)

The 'feigned madness' of both Žižek and the Joker acts as an antidote for the cynicism of the noble lies that conventional society is built upon. This makes the culmination of *The Dark Knight* such an unusually direct statement of capitalist ideology. Žižek and the Joker share an antic disposition that is designed to highlight, by contrast, the highly rationalized obtuseness with which society refuses to face up to its structuring verities. In fact and fiction, these provocateurs share the status of being beyond the pale of acceptable discourse. The marginal status that not only they but, by the end of *The Dark Knight*, Batman also assumes demonstrates in its form the content of their argument: that society requires subjective scapegoats to avoid confronting its own systemic truths – the objective violence it obscures through a distorting emphasis upon its subjective counterpart. Media critics of Žižek make use of constituted ideology to the extent that they indulge in similar sorts of distortions of his conceptual content. They also rely upon constituent ideology in their portrayals of him as a jester, a jokey nihilist. This is at the root of Žižek's mislabelling as a postmodern relativist. An establishment anxious about the potential unmasking of society's noble lies displaces that anxiety by ridiculing the joker's ridiculous jokes. However, whilst Žižek the joker and the Joker share a methodology, Žižek's consistent commitment to his interpretation of political truth (and its clear recognition of the relationship between the enunciated content and the position of the enunciator) distinguishes him from the nihilism of both the Joker and the political system he seeks to unmask. The truly nihilist approach is one in which constituent ideological practices are used to reduce essential political and social problems down to excessively subjective, caricatured distractions.

The Batman films raise serious ideological issues, but only in a manner that typifies Hollywood's adeptness at creating the conditions for capitalism's political somnambulism – we know very well that the bankers have bankrupted the system, but even so . . . These films are thus mythical anti-myths – in the guise of a myth they reinforce the pragmatic cynicism of everyday capitalism. Despite an initial portrayal of society's systemic internal contradictions, they reduce capitalism's structural problems to a faux-humanized battle between good and evil pantomime characters. The exaggerated forms those entities assume – a man-bat and a psychotic clown – have enough symbolic resonance to give the film a forebodingly dark thematic patina. Ultimately, however, legitimate concern about systemic cruelty is desublimated into the personalized figure of the Joker and, correspondingly, any notion of systemic justice is sublimated into the alienated subject of the batman imago – an individual figure prepared to suffer calumny for the 'greater good'. The dishonesty of the noble lie rests in defining the greater good as the maintenance of a system that actually serves the interests of a lesser minority. The essence of an ideological situation needs to be understood in terms of the form it assumes. To disentangle form and content, a mode of theoretically informed bracketing is required. Theory needs to counter for the very 'real abstraction' by which ideology works: for example, to compensate for the manner in which 'the abstraction from power and economic relations is inscribed into the very actuality of the democratic process' (*Parallax*: 56).

The truths of mass culture are artificially bracketed out from consideration as ideology in action by their status as 'just fiction'. *The Dark Knight*'s concluding evocation of the noble lie upon which capitalist culture relies represents an unusually explicit acknowledgement of how things really work. The importance of this statement should not be overlooked just because it is found within a fictional format. To avoid the difficulties of those trying to find a purloined letter hidden by the obviousness of its hiding place, or a dead body upon a battlefield, Žižek's solution lies in taking mass culture more seriously than it takes itself. To explore the interrelationship between the abstract and the real, masks and social reality, Žižek uses jokes and apparently facetious examples from the mass media, but whilst the Joker, portrayed so demonically by Jack Nicholson and Heath Ledger, has a passion for violence that merely represents the flip-side of capitalism's 'creative gales of destruction', Žižek is a joker with a deeply serious political point. Despite the humour along the way, his ultimate political point is no laughing matter – to paraphrase Police Commissioner James Gordon: 'Žižek is the theory-hero Gotham doesn't deserve . . . but the one it needs right now. So we'll hunt him, because he can take it. Because he's not our hero . . . he's a voluble guardian, a watchful provocateur . . . a dark knight of the dark night of the soul.'

CONCLUSION

Don't Just Do It: Negative Dialectics in the Age of Nike

Repressive intolerance toward a thought not immediately accompanied by instructions for action is founded in fear. ... An aged bourgeois mechanism with which the men of the Enlightenment of the eighteenth century were very familiar displays itself anew but unchanged: suffering caused by a negative condition ... turns into anger toward the person who expresses it ... becomes rage levelled at the person who expresses it. . . . Pseudo-activity is allied with pseudo-reality in the design of a subjective position; an activity that overplays itself and fires itself up for the sake of its own publicity without admitting to what degree it serves as a substitute for satisfaction, thus elevating itself to an end in itself. ... Within absolutized praxis, only reaction is possible and for this reason the reaction is false. ... When the doors are barricaded, it is doubly important that thought not be interrupted. (Adorno 2001 [1978]: 200)

The above excerpt from Theodor Adorno's short essay 'Resignation' succinctly conveys not only part of the anti-intellectual rationale of those wont to inveigh against Žižek, but also a key element of Žižek's counter-intuitive, perverted, defence of inactive theory as the best course of action when faced with the media's barrage of spectacles – its demand for its audience to engage in pseudo-activity, to act *now*. Adorno's argument resonates with Žižek's explanation of the 2005 riots in the Parisian *banlieues*. For Žižek, the rioters acted as unwitting collaborators in the production of the (in)effective non-politics of the spectacle – the pre-emptively co-opted, politically unfocused equivalent of Nike's advertising slogan *Just Do It*. The untargeted destruction by the rioters of their own local environment constituted 'phatic communication' – an impotent acting out. The made-for-media quality of the riots represented the foreclosure of genuine political protest:

> There were no particular demands made by the protestors in the Paris suburbs. There was only an insistence on *recognition*, based on vague, unarticulated *ressentiment*. Most of those interviewed talked about how unacceptable it was that the then interior minister, Nicolas Sarkozy, had called them 'scum'. In a weird self-referential short-circuit, they were protesting against the very reaction to their protests. ... what we have here is a zero-level protest, a violent protest act which demands nothing. (*Violence*: 64)

In the light of the global credit crisis, Žižek re-engineers the Clintonite political slogan 'it's the economy, stupid' into 'It's Ideology, Stupid!' (*Tragedy*: 9). He uses the reflexive ability of philosophy to recalibrate our 'commonsense' notion of the pragmatic worldliness of financial speculation when compared with its supposedly impractical otherworldly philosophical counterpart. Interpreting the *banlieues* riots as the ideological flip-side of the nominally non-violent acts of investment bankers, one can rephrase Žižek's above account: 'In a weird self-referential short-circuit, financiers were speculating against the very reaction to their speculations. . . . what we have here is an exponentially destructive level of speculation, a peaceful act of speculation which demands a huge government bail-out.'

Financial markets crash when beliefs about other people's beliefs spin out of control, just as the *banlieues* rioters lost control in response to their perception of Sarkozy's perception that the rest of France was simply not perceiving them as viable *citoyens de la République*. Both bankers and rioters embody *in extremis* a pervasive social phenomenon: our media-sponsored urge to be doing rather than talking. Philosophical analysis in both its mode of engagement (detached reflection) and its substantive content (ideologically sensitive concepts) provides a powerful practical alternative to the self-defeating nature of responding for the sake of being seen to respond – the pseudo-activity perhaps most vividly demonstrated by Bob Geldof's angry demand on UK TV during the Live Aid appeal: 'People are dying NOW. Give us the money NOW. Give me the money now.' A demand then followed by a rejection of a co-presenter's attempt to read out a postal address for donations: 'Fuck the address, just give the phone . . . here's the number . . . .' In contrast to such impatience, Žižek recalls a letter Marx wrote to Engels in 1870 in which, with revolution apparently at the gates of Europe, Marx complained about the revolutionaries' failure to wait until he had finished writing *Das Kapital* (*Violence*: 6). Rather than considering philosophy's otherworldly lack of immediacy as a drawback, it is exactly what the 'real world' needs:

The old saying 'Don't just talk, do something!' is one of the most stupid things one can say, even measured by the low standards of common sense. Perhaps, rather, the problem lately has been that we have been doing too much, such as intervening in nature, destroying the environment, and so forth. . . . Perhaps it is time to step back, think and *say* the right thing. True we often talk about something instead of doing it; but sometimes we also do things in order to avoid talking and thinking about them. Such as throwing $700 billion at a problem instead of reflecting on how it arose in the first place. (*Tragedy*: 11)

The media is symbolically most violent when it presents itself as a neutral conduit for reporting actual physical violence like the *banlieues* riots. That explicit *subjective* violence is presented with a misleading sense of urgency. Misleading because the very urgency with which you the viewer/listener are asked to respond is the very thing that will prevent you from recognizing the causes (*objective* violence) of the scenario you are witnessing.

The political mistake of the Parisian rioters was to feed into the media's essential grammar: the constant urgency that forms the background standard against which radio and TV current affairs programmes communicate. Contributors are constantly encouraged to express themselves with fluent speed instead of depth since profound problems need to be encapsulated for listeners 'in a nutshell'. The combined effect of the media's working grammar on any issue and the particular mode of presenting violent events from around the world create

the fake sense of urgency that pervades the left-liberal humanitarian discourse on violence: in it, abstraction and graphic (pseudo)concreteness coexist in the staging of the

scene of violence against women, blacks, the homeless, gays.
. . . 'A woman is raped every six seconds in this country' and
'In the time it will takes to read this paragraph, ten children
will die of hunger' are just two examples. . . . There is a fun-
damental anti-theoretical edge to these urgent injunctions.
There is no time to reflect: we have to *act now*. (*Violence*: 5–6)

Today, protesters, consumers, 'expert' financial commentators, and media reporters are all caught up within a realm
of caducean commercialism whereby commodity culture
intimately entwines itself with media technologies of the
spectacle. The ideological effect is a dampening down of
potentially critical reactions as the particular substantive
political issues contained within a scenario are flattened
out into the universal category of the mediated spectacle.
Rejecting the call to pseudo-action and advocating more
thought about causalities, Žižek's uses his short-circuit
juxtapositions of mass culture with philosophical and psychoanalytically fuelled insights to create his on-going project
of *looking awry* and adopting a *parallax view* – a mode of critical thought that offers at least a glimpse of a way out of the
self-referential, closed circuits of capitalist media.

THE IMP OF MOTIONLESS PERVERSITY

If we are successful we enable the patient *to abandon
invulnerability and to become a sufferer*. If we succeed life
becomes precarious to one who was beginning to know
a kind of stability and freedom from pain, even if this
meant non-participation in life and perhaps mental defect.
(Winnicott cited in Thompson 1994: 269)

Perversely, Žižek is criticized for being a joker *and* a pes-
simistic theorist who lacks ready solutions. We have also

seen throughout these pages, however, that underneath
Žižek's humour and refusal to offer solutions for the sake
of a (distinctly non-Kantian) purposefulness without purpose lies an admirable, non-relativist commitment to the
analytic attitude – true openness to life's complexities
achieved through absolute candour. By contrast, devotees
of the castration complacency complex, whose actions range
from removing dog testicles from an election campaign to
eliminating the word 'university' from the UK government
department responsible for education, seek to conceal rather
than uncover. When necessary, the services of the big Other
are enrolled so that we, the audience, do not have to confront
the nitty-gritty truth of a situation head-on. In *Casablanca*, as
previously described, we are allowed to fantasize in bad faith
as, formally, Rick and Ilsa didn't do it. Similarly, in Tiger
Woods' Nike-sponsored *mea culpa*, the all-too-public knowledge that he spent an impressive amount of energy precisely
just doing it is sublimated into a Hamlet-like conversation
with his father. The golf-player within the media's publicity play is discorporated into Nike's public relations play.
The conscience of the audience is not caught but distracted.
Nike's 'Just Do It' corporately invokes mindless participation to hide the mentally defective nature of a commodified
version of Winnicott's above notion of non-participation in
life.

   Hegel wrote that 'the man who flees is not yet free: in
fleeing he is still conditioned by that from which he flees'
(Hegel 1830: section 94). Developing this sentiment further,
Foucault claims:

> Our age ... is attempting to flee Hegel. ... But truly to
> escape Hegel involves an exact appreciation of the price
> we have to pay to detach ourselves from him. ... We have
> to determine the extent to which our anti-Hegelianism is

possibly one of his tricks directed against us, at the end of
which he stands, motionless, waiting for us. (Foucault 1972:
235)

Žižek's omnivorous appetite for both esoteric thought and
the mass media's crudest/schmaltziest content is not only
highly entertaining, it also proves to be much more effective at protecting theory than Hannah Arendt's alternative
described in the Introduction: centuries of oblivion and
neglect. In a capitalist media discourse that rejects the lost
causes of psychoanalysis and philosophy (whilst skilfully
incorporating into its everyday psychopathology some of
their keenest insights), like *Hamlet*'s Marcellus, Žižek stubbornly counsels against resorting to an uncritical and violent
acting out: 'We do it wrong, being so majestical, / To offer
it the show of violence; / For it is, as the air, invulnerable, /
And our vain blows malicious mockery' (Act I, Sc. i). More
optimistically, Žižek's work represents an equally stubborn
insistence that, no matter how much the media attempts to
flee theory's revelatory critical nature, even at the end of the
most frenetic Hollywood blockbuster, reality TV show, situation comedy, or ingenious advertisement, theory still stands
there motionless, waiting for us . . .

NOTES

Preface: The Dog's Bollocks . . . at the Media Dinner Party
1 Of Anglo-Saxon origin, 'bollocks' is British slang for 'testicles'. 'The dog's bollocks' is used to denote someone or something deemed to be admirable, as in 'the bee's knees' or 'the cat's pyjamas'.
2 Žižek offers a spirited defence of the legitimacy of using this particular joke approximately 37 minutes into this public talk (*http://www.youtube.com/watch?v=_GD69Cc20rw*).
3 The Greek word for dog (*kyon*) is the origin of the kynic (or Cynic) tradition of Diogenes. As a Situationist performer *avant la lettre*, Diogenes shocked the Athenian *agora* with such acts as public defecation and masturbation.

Introduction: 'The Marx Brother', 'The Elvis of Cultural
        Theory', and Other Media Clichés
1 Žižek on 'stretching a concept' (2004e website); Žižek on toilet design (2004d website).

2 For example, see the 2008 encounter between Žižek and Lévy at New York Public Library (*http://www. intelligencesquared.com/talks/violence-and-left-in-dark-times-bernard-henri-levy-and-slavoj-zizek*).

Chapter 1 The Mediated Imp of the Perverse

1 'From Heaven, across the world, to Hell' – Goethe, *Faust*.

2 Although it must be acknowledged that notions such as 'disproportionate' implicitly rely upon certain judgemental values that psychoanalysis has long struggled to remove totally from its use of the term (see Nobus 2006).

3 According to Žižek: '. . . acting out is a spectacle addressing a figure of the big Other, which leaves the big Other undisturbed in its place, while the *passage à l'acte* is a violent explosion which destroys the symbolic link itself' (*Living*: 326).

Chapter 2 Žižek's Tickling Shtick

1 I would like to thank David Thom for bringing this homophonic point to my attention.

2 From *The Expression of the Emotions in Man and Animals*, cited in Phillips 1994: 1.

3 The original photograph can be viewed here: *http:// faketurkey.blogspot.com/2009/04/fake-turkey-comes-full-cir cle.html* The further symbolic interpretation of the UK political cartoonist Stephen Bell is available here: *http:// www.guardian.co.uk/cartoons/stevebell/0,7371,1099119,00. html*. Finally, a toy entitled Turkey Dinner George Bush Doll was made to commemorate the incident and can be purchased from various online US outlets.

4 See Zupančič (2008) for a further iteration of this theme: Charlie Chaplin's performance in *Gold Rush* of a man who knows how to act like a chicken.

5   The article is inaccurately accompanied by a still photo-
    graph of Žižek on Bodega Bay taken from the unrelated
    TV series *The Pervert's Guide to Cinema*.
6   For more on this theme see Zupančič 2006 and 2008.
7   I would like to thank Prof. David J. Gunkel for
    his insights on the relationship between *Curb Your
    Enthusiasm* and *Seinfeld*.

Chapter 3 Big (Br)Other: Psychoanalysing the Media
1   The non-fictional reality of this filmic depiction is artic-
    ulated in Fénelon 1977.
2   I would like to thank Prof. David J. Gunkel for
    his insights on Žižek's interpretations of Kant and
    Hegel.
3   See Taylor and Harris 2008 for a discussion of this
    theme in relation to the notion of 'Banality TV'.

*Chapter 4 Understanding Media: The Sublime Objectification
of Ideology*
1   See Goldman and Papson 1998.
2   The psychotic patient typically presents with language
    disorders that

> are due to the psychotic's lack of a sufficient
> number of anchoring points: the psychotic experi-
> ence is characterized by a constant slippage of the
> signifier under the signified, which is a disaster for
> signification. Later, Lacan will posit that there is
> a continual 'cascade of reshapings of the signifier
> from which the increasing disaster of the imagi-
> nary proceeds, until the level is reached at which
> signifier and signified are stabilized in the delu-
> sional metaphor.' Thus 'the nucleus of psychosis
> has to be linked to a rapport between the subject
> and the signifier in its most formal dimension, in its

dimension as pure signifier. If the neurotic inhabits language, the psychotic is inhabited, possessed by language.' (Lacan 2009)

3 Discussed in detail in Fried 2007.
4 In a manner reminiscent of Heidegger's distinction between the mutual indebtedness of the Aristotelian four causes and modernity's exclusionary focus upon only the technology-centred *causa efficiens* – see his essay 'The Question Concerning Technology' (Heidegger 1954).
5 It is also reminiscent of a series of adverts for the UK instant coffee Mellow Birds. Available at: *http://www. youtube.com/watch?v=uqAu5w5fhvI*

Chapter 5 The Media's Violence

1 Cited in Žižek 2006c website.
2 Originally broadcast on BBC2 at 20:00 on 11 July 2009.
3 Originally broadcast on Channel 4 at 20:00 on 3 August 2009 as part of the channel's Street Weapons Commission (see *http://www.channel4.com/news/microsites /S/street_weapons_commission/index.html*).
4 *http://www.fair.org/index.php?page=1084*
5 David Kelly was a government scientist who committed suicide after being caught up in the political fall-out that resulted from the dissemination of the 2003 'dodgy dossier': a briefing document containing retrospectively inaccurate claims about the imminent nature of Iraq's missile threat that the British Government used as part of its justification for joining the Allied invasion.
6 From the director's commentary soundtrack of the documentary film *Standard Operating Procedure* (2008).

7 For Tony Blair's reported outrage at footage of dead British soldiers, see Macintyre 2003 and Miles 2003; and for criticism for showing both US and UK dead soldiers, see Mail Online undated.

8 For this story of callous indifference that was reported in the world's media, see Hooper 2008; also Žižek 2009c website. For a similar, more factual article on the specific juxtaposition of Lampedusa and African immigration, see Popham 2006.

9 The two pictures in question and discussion of their ideological implications are available at de Moraes 2005, Kinney 2005, and Media Awareness Network undated.

10 Available at: *http://www.youtube.com/watch?v=9pVTrnx CZaQ* and: *http://www.spike.com/video/kanye-west-attacks/ 2678975*

11 This interview can be accessed here: *http://www.youtube. com/watch?v=KjEtmZZvGZA&feature=related*

12 In his seminal essay 'The Triumph of Mass Idols', Leo Lowenthal (1961) identifies a shift in the cultural focus of the mass media from 'idols of consumption' to 'idols of production' that began in the inter-war years.

13 For example, the *ad hominem* criticism of Julian Baggini (2008).

14 Cited in *Violence*: 33.

Chapter 6 The Joker's Little Shop of Ideological Horrors

1 In a typically mischievous move, Adam Kirsch's accusation that Žižek is 'the most dangerous philosopher in the West' (Kirsch 2009) is used as an advertising byline on the front of *Living in the End Times*.

2 See Adam Kirsch's (2008) review of *In Defence of Lost Causes*.

3 A similar illustration of this relationship between

fiction's ability to pre-emptively account for socially traumatic trends can be seen from the prescience of Morgan Robertson's 1898 novella *Futility, Or The Wreck of the Titan*, which prefigured the Titanic's sinking in 1912.

BIBLIOGRAPHY

Books by Žižek

Borrowed Kettle = *The Borrowed Kettle.* London: Verso, 2004.

Desert = *Welcome to the Desert of the Real.* London: Verso, 2002.

Fragile Absolute = *The Fragile Absolute, or Why the Christian Legacy is Worth Fighting For.* London: Verso, 2000.

How to Read Lacan = *How to Read Lacan.* London: Granta Books, 2006.

Indivisible Remainder = *The Indivisible Remainder: An Essay on Schelling and Related Matters.* London: Verso, 1996.

Living = *Living in the End Times.* London: Verso, 2010.

Looking Awry = *Looking Awry: An Introduction to Jacques Lacan Through Popular Culture.* London: MIT Press, 1991.

Lost Causes = *In Defence of Lost Causes.* London: Verso, 2008.

On Belief = *On Belief.* New York: Routledge, 2001.

Organs = *Organs without Bodies: Deleuze and Consequences.* London: Routledge, 2003.

Parallax = *The Parallax View*. Cambridge, MA: MIT Press, 2006.

Plague = *The Plague of Fantasies*. London: Verso, 1997.

Puppet = *The Puppet and the Dwarf: The Perverse Core of Christianity*. Cambridge, MA: MIT Press, 2002.

Real Tears = *The Fright of Real Tears: Krzysztof Kieślowski between Theory and Post-Theory*. Bloomington: Indiana University Press, 2001.

Robespierre = (ed.) *Slavoj Žižek presents Robespierre: Virtue and Terror*. London: Verso, 2007.

Sublime Object = *The Sublime Object of Ideology*. London: Verso, 1989.

Symptom = *Enjoy Your Symptom! Jacques Lacan in Hollywood and Out*. London: Routledge, 1992; second edition, 2001.

Tarrying = *Tarrying with the Negative: Kant, Hegel and the Critique of Ideology*. Durham, NC: Duke University Press, 1993.

They Know = *For They Know Not What They Do: Enjoyment as a Political Factor*. London: Verso, 1991.

Ticklish Subject = *The Ticklish Subject: The Absent Centre of Political Ontology*. London: Verso, 1999.

Totalitarianism = *Did Somebody Say Totalitarianism? Five Essays in the (Mis)Use of a Notion*. London: Verso, 2001.

Tragedy = *First as Tragedy, Then as Farce*. London: Verso, 2009.

Violence = *Violence: Six Sideways Reflections*. London: Profile Books, 2008.

Žižek Website Material

Undated 'The Village'. Available at: *http//www.theperverts-guide.com/extras_zizek_thevillage.html*

1997a 'The Big Other Doesn't Exist'. *JEP*, No. 5, Spring–Fall 1997. Available at: *http://www.psychomedia.it/jep/number5/zizek.htm*

1997b 'From Joyce-the-Symptom to the Symptom of Power'. *Lacanian Ink*. Available at: *http://www.plexus.org/lacink/lacink11/zizek.html*

1997c 'How to Read Lacan. 2: Empty Gestures and Performatives: Lacan Confronts the CIA Plot'. Available at: *http://www.lacan.com/zizciap.html*

1998 'The Interpassive Subject'. Centre Georges Pompidou, Traverses. Available at: *http://www.lacan.com/zizek-pompidou.htm*

2001 'Welcome to the Desert of the Real'. Available at: *http://web.mit.edu/cms/reconstructions/interpretations/desert real.html*

2004a 'What Rumsfeld Doesn't Know That He Knows About Abu Ghraib'. Available at: *http://www.lacan.com/zizekrumsfeld.htm*

2004b 'A Cup of Decaf Reality'. Available at: *http://www.lacan.com/zizekdecaf.htm*

2004c 'Between Two Deaths: The Culture of Torture'. *London Review of Books*, 3 June. Available at: *http://www.lacan.com/zizek torture.htm*

2004d 'Knee-Deep (Review of Timothy Garton Ash's *Free World*)'. *London Review of Books*, 2 September. Available at: *http://www.lrb.co.uk/v26/n17/print/zize01_.html*

2004e 'The Ongoing Soft Revolution'. *Critical Inquiry*, Winter. Available at: *http://www.lacan.com/zizek-inquiry1.html*

2005a 'The Act and its Vicissitudes'. Available at: *http://www.lacan.com/symptom6_articles/zizek.html*

2005b 'Some Politically Incorrect Reflections on Violence in France & Related Matters'. Available at: *http://www.lacan.com/zizfrance4.htm*

2005c 'With or Without Passion, What's Wrong with Fundamentalism? – Part I'. Available at: *http://www.lacan.com/zizpassion.htm*

2006a 'Nobody Has to be Vile'. *London Review of Books*, 6 April. Available at: *http://www.lrb.co.uk/v28/n07/slavoj-zizek/nobody-has-to-be-vile*

2006b 'Freud Lives'. *London Review of Books*, 25 May. Available at: *http://www.lrb.co.uk/v28/n10/slavoj-zizek/freud-lives*

2006c 'The Antinomies of Tolerant Reason: A Blood-Dimmed Tide is Loosed'. Available at: *http://www.lacan.com/zizantinomies.htm*

2007a 'Shostakovich in Casablanca'. Available at: *http://www.lacan.com/zizcasablanca.htm*

2007b 'How to Read Lacan From Che Vuoi? to Fantasy: Lacan with Eyes Wide Shut'. Available at: *http://www.lacan.com/zizkubrick.htm*

2009a 'Capitalism, Healthcare, Latin American "Populism" and the "Farcical" Financial Crisis'. Video interview on *Democracy Now!* Both footage and transcript available at: *http://www.democracynow.org/2009/10/15/slovenian_philosopher_slavoj_zizek_on_the*

2009b 'Hollywood Today: Report from an Ideological Frontline'. Available at: *http://www.lacan.com/essays/?page_id=347*

2009c 'Berlusconi in Tehran'. *London Review of Books*, 23 July. Available at: *http://www.lrb.co.uk/v31/n14/zize01_.html?utm_source=newsletter&utm_medium=email&utm_campaign=3114*

Other Works

Adorno, T.W. (2001) *The Culture Industry: Selected Essays on Mass Culture* (ed. J.M. Bernstein). London: Routledge.

Arendt, H. (1982) *Lectures on Kant's Political Philosophy*. Cicago: University of Chicago Press.

Arendt, H. (1993 [1954]) *Between Past and Future: Eight Exercises in Political Thought*. London: Penguin.

Arendt, H. (1994 [1951]) *The Origins of Totalitarianism*. New York: Harcourt Inc.

Bacevich, A.J. (2008) 'He Told Us to Go Shopping. Now the Bill is Due', *The Washington Post*, 5 October. Available at: *http://www.washingtonpost.com/wp-dyn/content/article/2008/10/03/AR2008100301977.html*

Baggini, J. (2008) 'Book of the Week: Violence by Slavoj Žižek'. *Times Higher Education*, 14 February. Available at: *http://www.timeshighereducation.co.uk/story.asp?storycode=400599*

Barthes, R. (1973) *Mythologies*. London: Paladin Books.

Baudrillard, J. (2002) *The Spirit of Terrorism*. London: Verso.

Bearn, M. (2004) 'On the Rampage'. *New Statesman*, 2 August. Available at: *http://www.newstatesman.com/200408020033*

Benjamin, W. (1936) 'The Work of Art in the Age of Mechanical Reproduction'. Available at: *http://www.marxists.org/reference/subject/philosophy/works/ge/benjamin.htm*

Boorstin, D. (1992 [1961]) *The Image: A Guide to Pseudo-Events in America*. New York: Vintage.

Bowman, P. and Stamp, R. (2007) *The Truth of Žižek*. London. Continuum.

Channel 4 News (2009) 'Did Mandelson Use the "Chump" Word?' Available at: *http://www.channel4.com/news/articles/politics/domestic_politics/did+mandelson+use+the+aposchumpapos+word/3366597*

Chesterton, G.K. (2004 [1911]) 'The Sign of the Broken Sword'. Available at: *http://books.eserver.org/fiction/innocence/brokensword.html*

Clark, A. (2009) 'When is a Starbucks Not a Starbucks?' *Guardian*, 22 July. Available at: *http://www.guardian.co.uk/lifeandstyle/2009/jul/22/starbucks*

CNN (2008) 'Jackson Apologizes for "Crude" Obama Remarks'. Available at: *http://edition.cnn.com/2008/POLITICS/07/09/jesse.jackson.comment/*

Collateral Murder (2010) Video – Transcript. Available at: *http://www.collateralmurder.com/en/transcript.html*

Danchev, A. (2005) 'Story Development, or Walter Mitty the Undefeated', in A. Danchev and J. Macmillan (eds) *The Iraq War and Democratic Politics*. London: Routledge.

Davies, M.L. (1996) 'University Culture or Intellectual Culture?' in B. Brecher, O. Fleischmann, and J. Halliday (eds) *The University in a Liberal State*. Aldershot: Avebury.

de Moraes, L. (2005) 'Kanye West's Torrent of Criticism, Live on NBC'. *The Washington Post*, 3 September. Available at: *http://www.washingtonpost.com/wp-dyn/content/ article/2005/09/03/AR2005090300165.html*

Debord, G. (1977 [1967]) *The Society of the Spectacle*. Detroit, MI: Black and Red.

Derbyshire, J. (2009) 'I am a Leninist. Lenin Wasn't Afraid to Dirty His Hands. If You Can Get Power, Grab It'. *New Statesman*, 29 October. Available at: *http://www.newstates man.com/ideas/2009/11/381-382-interview-obama-theory*

Eagleton, T. (2003) *After Theory*. London: Allen Lane.

Fénelon, F. (1977) *The Musicians of Auschwitz*. London: Michael Joseph.

Fisher, M. (2006) 'Gothic Oedipus: Subjectivity and Capitalism in Christopher Nolan's *Batman* Begins'. *ImageTexT: Interdisciplinary Comics Studies*, Vol. 2, No. 2 (Winter). Available at: *http://www.english.ufl.edu/imagetext/ archives/v2_2/fisher/*

Foucault, M. (1972) 'The Discourse on Language', in *Archaeology of Knowledge and The Discourse on Language*. New York: Pantheon.

Freud, S. (2001a [1900]). *The Interpretation of Dreams (I)* (ed. J. Strachey). The Standard Edition of the Complete Psychological Works, Vol. IV. London: Vintage.

Freud, S. (2001b [1901]) *The Psychopathology of Everyday Life* (ed. J. Strachey). The Standard Edition of the Complete Psychological Works, Vol. VI. London: Vintage.

Freud, S. (2001c [1901–5]) *A Case of Hysteria, Three Essays on Sexuality and Other Works* (ed. J. Strachey). The Standard Edition of the Complete Psychological Works, Vol. VII. London: Vintage.

Freud, S. (2001d [1905]) *Jokes and Their Relation to the Unconscious* (ed. J. Strachey). The Standard Edition of the Complete Psychological Works, Vol. VIII. London: Vintage.

Freud, S. (2001e [1911–13]) *'The Case of Schreber', 'Papers on Technique' and Other Works* (ed. J. Strachey). The Standard Edition of the Complete Psychological Works, Vol. XII. London: Vintage.

Freud, S. (2001f [1923–5]) *The Ego and the Id* (ed. J. Strachey). The Standard Edition of the Complete Psychological Works, Vol. XIX. London: Vintage.

Freud, S. (2003 [1899–1919]) *The Uncanny*. London: Penguin.

Fried, G. (2007) 'Where's the Point? Slavoj Žižek and the Broken Sword'. *International Journal of Žižek Studies*, Vol. 1, No. 4. Available at: *http://zizekstudies.org/index.php/ijzs/article/viewFile/83/146*

Gabriel, M. and Žižek, S. (2009) *Mythology, Madness and Laughter: Subjectivity in German Idealism*. London: Continuum.

Goldman, R. and Papson, S. (1998) *Nike Culture: The Sign of the Swoosh*. London: Sage Publications.

Gramsci, A. (1971) *Selections from the Prison Notebooks of Antonio Gramsci* (ed. Q. Hoare and G. Nowell Smith). London: Lawrence and Wishart.

Guardian Mediamonkey (2009) 'Lord Mandelson Blames a Bad Line for "Swearing" at the Sun'. 30 September.

Available at:*http://www.guardian.co.uk/media/mediamonkey-blog/2009/sep/30/sun-peter-mandelson*

Hari, J. (2007) 'The Star Philosopher Slavoj Žižek Commits Intellectual Suicide in His Latest Film'. Available at: *http://www.newstatesman.com/film/2007/04/slavoj-zizek-inte llectual*

Hari, J. (2009) 'Superwoman Falls to Earth'. *The Independent Arts Supplement 13*, 2 November. Available at: *http://www.slate.com/?id=2233966*

Hegel, G.W.F. (1830) *The Encylopedia of Philosophical Sciences: Part One. The Logic.* Available at: *http://www.marxists.org/reference/archive/hegel/works/sl/slbeing.htm*

Hegel, G.W.F. (1977 [1807]) *The Phenomenology of Spirit.* Oxford: Oxford University Press.

Heidegger, M. (1954) *The Question Concerning Technology.* Available at: *http://www.wright.edu/cola/Dept/PHL/Class/P.Internet/PITexts/QCT.html*

Hill, M.A. (1979) 'On Hannah Arendt', in M.A. Hill (ed.), *Hannah Arendt: The Recovery of the Public World.* New York: St Martin's Press.

Hooper, J. (2008) 'Gypsy Girls' Corpses on Beach in Italy Fail to Put Off Sunbathers'. *Guardian*, 21 July. Available at: *http://www.guardian.co.uk/world/2008/jul/21/italy.race*

Huffington Post (2009) 'Interracial Couple Denied Marriage License by Louisiana Justice of the Peace'. Available at: *http://www.huffingtonpost.com/2009/10/15/interracial-couple-denied_n_322784.html*

Huntington, S.P. (1996) *The Clash of Civilizations and the Remaking of World Order.* London: Simon & Schuster.

Jameson, F. (1992) *Postmodernism or, The Cultural Logic of Late Capitalism.* London: Verso.

Jay, M. (1996 [1973]). *The Dialectical Imagination: A History of the Frankfurt School and the Institute of Social Research 1923–1950.* Berkeley, CA: University of California Press.

Kant, I. (1965 [1781]) *Critique of Pure Reason*. New York: St Martin's Press.

Kinney, A. (2005) '"Looting" or "Finding?"' *Salon.com*, 1 September. Available at: *http://dir.salon.com/story/news/feature/2005/09/01/photo_controversy/index.html*

Kirsch, A. (2008) 'The Deadly Jester'. *The New Republic*, 3 December. Available at: *http://www.tnr.com/article/books/the-deadly-jester*

Kirsch, A. (2009) 'Disputations: Still the Most Dangerous Philosopher in the West'. *The New Republic*, 7 January. Available at: *http://www.tnr.com/article/politics/disputations-still-the-most-dangerous-philosopher-the-west*

Kracauer, S. (1995) *The Mass Ornament: The Weimar Essays*. Cambridge, MA: Harvard University Press.

Kraus, K. (2001 [1923]) *Dicta and Contradicta*. Urbana and Chicago: University of Illinois Press.

Lacan, J. (2008) *My Teaching*. London: Verso.

Lacan, J., Miller, J.A., and Hulbert, J. (1977) 'Desire and the Interpretation of Desire in Hamlet'. *Yale French Studies*, No. 55/56, 'Literature and Psychoanalysis. The Question of Reading: Otherwise'. Available at: *http://www.wehavephotoshop.com/PHILOSOPHY%20NOW/PHILOSOPHY/Lacan/Jacques.Lacan.Desire.And.The.Interpretation.Of.Desire.In.Hamlet.pdf*

Lacan, J. (2009) *The Seminars of Jacques Lacan: Book III: The Psychoses*. Available at: *http://lacan.com/seminars1.htm*

Lewis, R. (2009) *Seasonal Suicide Notes*. London: Short Books.

Lezard, N. (2009) 'Something Rotten in Society? Time to Revive Communism'. *Guardian*, 24 October. *http://www.guardian.co.uk/books/2009/oct/24/tragedy-farce-slavoj-zizek-lezard*

Lowenthal, L. (1961) *Literature, Popular Culture & Society*. Palo Alto, CA: Pacific Books.

McGowan, T. (2007) 'Introduction: Enjoying the Cinema',

'Žižek and Cinema'. *International Journal of Žižek Studies*, Vol. 1, No. 3. Available at: *http://zizekstudies.org/index.php/ijzs/article/views/57/119*

Macintyre, D. (1999) 'Mandelson: The Push for Power'. *The Independent*, 23 April. Available at: *http://www.independent.co.uk/arts-entertainment/mandelson-the-push-for-power-1088976.html*

Macintyre, D. (2003) 'Blair's "Horror" over TV Footage of Dead Soldiers'. *The Independent*, 27 March. Available at: *http://www.independent.co.uk/news/world/middle-east/blairs-horror-over-tv-footage-of-dead-soldiers-592531.html*

McLuhan, M. (1995 [1964]) *Understanding Media: The Extensions of Man*. London: Routledge.

Mail Online (undated) 'Al-Jazeera Defends "Dead Allies" Video'. *Daily Mail*. Available at: *http://www.dailymail.co.uk/news/article-173981/Al-Jazeera-defends-dead-allies-video.html*

Mandelson, P. (2008) Letters Page. *Guardian*, 12 January. Available at: *http://www.guardian.co.uk/politics/2008/jan/12/tonyblair.labour*

Marcuse, H. (2002 [1964]) *One Dimensional Man*. London: Routledge. Available at: *http://www.marxists.org/reference/archive/marcuse/works/one-dimensional-man/index.htm*

Media Awareness Network (undated) 'Hurricane Katrina and the "Two-Photo" Controversy'. Available at: *http://www.media-awareness.ca/english/resources/educational/teachable_moments/katrina_2_photo.cfm*

Miles, H. (2003) 'Watching the War on al-Jazeera'. *London Review of Books*, 17 April. Available at: *http://www.lrb.co.uk/v25/n08/hugh-miles/watching-the-war-on-al-jazeera*

Mills, C.W. (2000 [1959]) *The Sociological Imagination*. Oxford: Oxford University Press.

Muller, J.P. (1980) 'Psychosis and Mourning in Lacan's Hamlet'. *New Literary History*, Vol. 12, No. 1, Psychology and Literature: Some Contemporary Directions (Autumn), pp. 147–65.

Muller, J.P. and Richardson, W.J. (1988) *The Purloined Poe: Lacan, Derrida, and Psychoanalytical Reading*. London: Johns Hopkins University Press.

Nobus, D. (2006) 'Introduction: Locating Perversion, Dislocating Psychoanalysis', in D. Nobus and L. Downing (eds) *Perversion: Psychoanalytic Perspectives/Perspectives on Psychoanalysis*. London and New York: Karnac Books.

O'Farrell, J. (2001) 'Farewell, Focus Groupie: What a Fuss About a Man Who Turned the Labour Party into an Airbrushed Bulldog'. *Guardian*, 27 January. Available at: *http://www.guardian.co.uk/politics/2001/jan/27/labour.man delson*

Phillips, A. (1994) *On Kissing, Tickling, and Being Bored: Psychoanalytic Essays on the Unexamined Life*. London: Verso.

Pickard, J. (2009) 'Tense Encounter between Lord Mandelson and The Sun'. *The Financial Times*, 30 September. Available at: *http://blogs.ft.com/westminster/2009 /09/tense-encounter-between-lord-mandelson-and-the-sun/*

Pilkington, E. (2009) 'Seinfeld Cast "Reunites" on HBO's Curb Your Enthusiasm'. *The Guardian*, 5 October. Available at: *http://www.guardian.co.uk/media/2009/oct/05/ seinfeld-curb-your-enthusiasm*

Poole, S. (2007) 'Postmodernists, Žižek and "Intellectual Suicide"'. Available at: *http://unspeak.net/postmodernists/*

Popham, P. (2006) 'Bodies of African Immigrants Pile Up Around Sunbathers'. *The Independent*, 16 May. Available at: *http://www.independent.co.uk/news/world/europe/bodies-of-african-immigrants-pile-up-around-sunbathers-478379.html*

Popham, P. (2007) 'Tunisian Fishermen Face 15 Years' Jail in Italy for Saving Migrants from Rough Seas'. *The Independent*, 20 September. Available at: *http://www.*

independent.co.uk/news/world/europe/tunisian-fishermen-face-15-years-jail-in-italy-for-saving-migrants-from-rough-seas-40 2907.html

Reece, C. (2008) 'Jokers Wild, or Batman Degree Zero: The Dark Knight'. Available at: *http://www.amoeba.com/ blog/2008/08/writings-from-the-holy-texan/joker-s-wild-or-bat man-degree-zero-the-dark-knight-2008-.html*

Rickels, L.A. (1990) 'Psychoanalysis on TV Author(s)'. *SubStance*, Vol. 19, No. 1, Issue 61: Special Issue: Voice-Over: On Technology, pp. 39–52.

Sartre, J.-P. (1983 [1938]) *Nausea*. London: Penguin.

Sartre, J.-P. (1966 [1943]) *Being and Nothingness*. New York: Simon & Schuster.

Sartre, J.-P. (2001 [1948]) *What is Literature?* London: Routledge.

Solnit, R. (2009) 'Four Years On, Katrina Remains Cursed by Rumour, Cliché, Lies and Racism'. *Guardian*, 26 August. Available at: *http://www.guardian.co.uk/commentisfree/2009/ aug/26/katrina-racism-us-media*

Szaz, T. (1990) *Anti-Freud: Karl Kraus's Criticism of Psychoanalysis and Psychiatry*. Syracuse, NY: Syracuse University Press.

Taylor, P.A. (2007) 'Baudrillard's Radical Media Theory and William Merrin's Baudrillard and the Media'. *International Journal of Baudrillard Studies*, Vol. 4, No. 1. Available at: *http://www.ubishos.ca/baudrillardstudies/vol4_1/taylorr.htm*

Taylor, P.A. (2008a) 'Perverted Research and the Political Imagination – The Trial of the Good Scholar Švejk'. *European Political Science*, Vol. 7, No. 3, pp. 335–51.

Taylor, P.A. (2008b) 'Baudrillard's Resistance to the Ob-scene as the Mis-en-Scene (Or, Refusing to Think Like a Lap-Dancer's Client)'. *International Journal of Baudrillard Studies*, Vol. 5, No. 2. Available at: *http://www. ubishops.ca/BaudrillardStudies/vol-5_2/v5-2-taylor.html*

Taylor, P.A. (2010) 'Totalitarian Bureaucracy and Bauman's Sociological Imagination – in Defence of the Ivory Tower', in M. Davis and K. Tester (eds) *Bauman's Challenge: Sociological Issues for the Twenty-First Century*. Basingstoke: Macmillan.

Taylor, P. A. and Harris, J.L. (2005) *Digital Matters: Theory and Culture of the Matrix*. London: Routledge.

Taylor, P. A. and Harris, J.L. (2008) *Critical Theories of Mass Media: Then and Now*. Maidenhead: Open University Press.

Thompson, A.C. (2009) 'New Evidence Surfaces in Post-Katrina Crimes'. *The Nation*, 11 July. Available at: *http://www.thenation.com/doc/20090720/thompson*

Thompson, M.G. (1994) *The Truth About Freud's Technique: The Encounter with the Real*. New York: New York University Press.

Thornhill, J. (2009) 'Lunch with the FT: Slavoj Žižek'. Available at: *http://ionalecsandru.blogspot.com/2009/03/lunch-with-ft-slavoj-zizek-by-john.html*

Wansink, B. and Cheney, M.M. (2005) 'Super Bowls: Serving Bowl Size and Food Consumption'. *The Journal of the American Medical Association (JAMA)*, Vol. 293, No. 14. Available at: *http://jama.ama-assn.org/cgi/content/full/293/14/1727*

Wintour, P. (2009) 'Simon Cowell Plans "Political X Factor"'. *Guardian*, 14 December. Available at: *http://www.guardian.co.uk/uk/2009/dec/14/cowell-plans-political-x-factor*

Wolin, R. (2004) *The Seduction of Unreason: The Intellectual Romance with Fascism from Nietzsche to Postmodernism*. Princeton: Princeton University Press.

Zupančič, A. (2006) 'Reversals of Nothing: The Case of the Sneezing Corpse'. *Filozofski Vestnik*. Available at: *http://filozof skivestnikonline.com/index.php/journal/article/view/12/32*

Zupančič, A. (2008) *The Odd One In: On Comedy*. Cambridge, MA: MIT Press.

INDEX